EXPERIMENTS IN HISTORY TEACHING

Experiments In History Teaching

edited by

STEPHEN BOTEIN
WARREN LEON
MICHAEL NOVAK
ROY ROSENZWEIG
G.B. WARDEN

published for

Harvard-Danforth Center for Teaching and Learning

The Press of The Langdon Associates

Cambridge, Massachusetts

1978

ACKNOWLEDGMENTS

Our largest and most obvious debt is to more than 75 New England history teachers, who wrote this book. Their example of generously sharing ideas, time, and energy — along with that of many others who participated in "Experiments in History Teaching" — is all too rare in a competitive profession.

Neither this publication nor the program from which it evolved would have been possible without a grant from the Harvard-Danforth Center for Teaching and Learning. We would like to thank the Director of the Center, Dean Whitla, and Administrative Assistant Karen Freeze for their encouragement over the past year. Nancy Cramer, Administrative Assistant of the Harvard History Department, was kind enough to handle our financial accounts. We are also obligated to the New England History Teachers' Association for their continuing support of this entire project, especially in its early organizational stages.

During the hectic months of editing, Kenneth Hodder and Jean Trescott provided able and diligent research assistance. Paul Tedesco, of Northeastern University, was kind enough to lend a large collection of history teaching materials from his personal library. Finally, we are grateful to Ann Orlov for guiding five novices through the intricacies of publishing.

Edith Read designed and supervised the production of this book. It was typeset by Phil Grueneich.

Second printing 1978
Published for the Harvard-Danforth Center for Teaching and Learning
Harvard University, Cambridge, Massachusetts 02138

by The Press of The Langdon Associates
41 Langdon Street
Cambridge, Massachusetts 02138

Manufactured in the United States of America by
Lithographic Publications, Inc., Stoneham, Massachusetts

Library of Congress Catalog Card Number: 77-148
ISBN 0-916704-03-3

PREFACE

Although ancient wisdom has it that teaching cannot be taught, experienced teachers usually have something to gain by exchanging ideas and materials among themselves. History teachers, at this particular moment in the history of their discipline, may have more to learn than most.

Whether or not the "crisis of relevance" so widely perceived at the end of the last decade has passed, professional alarm over student attitudes toward history seems lately to have subsided. But there is a more compelling reason for history teachers at the present time to pool their resources and collaborate in exploring solutions to common problems.

The contemporary world of historical scholarship is alive with discussion. One crucial challenge facing history teachers today is to communicate to students some understanding of the issues and concerns that are stirring up controversy among scholars and inspiring imaginative research. This is no easy task, in an era of increasingly specialized investigation. But if it is true that history teaching at all levels will benefit from being integrated with the methods, sources, and findings of recent scholarship, the moment seems right to experiment with new pedagogical approaches. The "new" historical scholarship (which of course has a history of its own) is now reasonably well established. Although its practitioners differ on theoretical points, generally this literature borrows methods from other disciplines, especially the social sciences, and is attentive to the experiences of people who have not figured prominently in traditional political narratives. How may the techniques and themes of the "new" history be brought into the classroom?

In 1976-1977, with this question in mind, a small group of Cambridge-based historians — who are the editors of this volume — organized a program at Harvard University called "Experiments in History Teaching." Supported by a modest grant from the Harvard-Danforth Center for Teaching and Learning, EHT consisted of a series of meetings throughout the year that brought together several hundred history teachers from a variety of institutions in the New England region. Speakers and workshop participants drew on their own class-room experiences to consider applications of the "new" history and other related scholarship to teaching. Five topics were chosen — "Cultural Artifacts," "Community History," "Personality in History," "History from the Bottom Up," and "Quantifying the Past" — that seemed to represent areas where recent scholarship and experimental teaching converged.

What follows is a collective effort to adapt for print numerous insights and examples offered at different sessions of EHT. Supplementary material has been added where appropriate. By design, this is an eclectic volume that reflects a multiplicity of perspectives. Individual contributors bear no responsibility for the views of others appearing in the same section or even on the same page, or for the overall editorial framework. The editors, for their part, have refrained from trying to impose any orthodoxy of approach on the miscellany of creative experimentation in New England that has been reported over the past year. A few editorial preliminaries, by way of disclaimer and summary, will suffice to introduce a volume that requires no apology for being merely — and precisely — the sum of its parts.

We want to emphasize, above all, that this is in no sense a comprehensive directory of innovative history teachers in New England. For one thing, logistics dictated that teachers in eastern Massachusetts would predominate at EHT meetings. Some who might have contributed were prevented from doing so because of schedule conflicts, sabbaticals, and the like. Naturally, too, limitations of space have made it necessary to select only a representative sampling of the various new approaches that history teachers have adopted in the region.

What this indicates, perhaps unsurprisingly, is that there are more experimental history teachers in New England than we originally realized. It is just a matter of knowing where to look. EHT took place at Harvard, physically, but on the whole experimental history teaching seems most vital in classrooms outside the ivory tower. To what extent history teachers in the region have been inspired by recent university scholarship is uncertain. Some, it appears, have developed new approaches on their own, even in anticipation of scholarly trends. Possibly, university faculty in history — from the toilsome nature of their research — lag behind other teachers in adapting new ideas from the larger intellectual world to the study of the past. But whatever the explanation, history teachers in high schools and community colleges definitely have much to offer those teaching at other educational levels. This suggests that if history teachers are to work productively together, they should try to surmount the system of rivalries and distinctions that divides their profession by categories of institution and scholarly specialty.

In addition to presenting a multi-institutional regional model of educational collaboration, it is the aim of this volume to stimulate further experimentation by history teachers — in New England and elsewhere. This is not to insist, however, that novelty is always preferable to what has often proven serviceable in the past. All of us know outstanding history teachers who choose to lecture, most traditionally and most effectively, on kings, battles, and other unfashionable subjects. They are unrepresented here not because their approach is unappealing but because it is already thoroughly familiar. Let it be further understood, in this context, that experiments in history teaching often fail. Perhaps no quality is more important in an experimental history teacher than courage — the courage to try and err, in the face of a visibly skeptical class.

Lastly, we should warn readers to expect little educational theory within this volume. It will be obvious enough that our editorial sympathies lie not only with the goals of the "new" history but with the premises of teaching that involves students in the process of first-hand investigation. This raises large difficult issues, however, much debated in certain quarters. Such matters we will leave to others. The five topical units in what follows are broadly conceived, in accordance with the structure of a year-long program that deliberately but uneasily balanced discussion of substance and demonstration of method, without ever systematizing the questions and answers formulated by different participants.

This is a volume that we would like to think will reward random perusal, if not more sustained study. To borrow a figure of speech from a regional poet named Frost, it is our hope that as the reader wanders through these pages a few ideas will stick — as burrs to clothing, in a tramp through densely wooded country.

S.B.
W.L.
M.N.
R.R.
G.B.W.

Cambridge, Massachusetts
October, 1977

TABLE OF CONTENTS

Cultural Artifacts

introduction

One challenge that history teachers always face is to bring students into imaginative contact with the values, traditions, and relationships of past societies. To show what different historical patterns of thought and interaction meant to those people whose lives were expressed through them, many teachers in the New England region have drawn on the sources and insights of what may be called the "new" cultural history.

Traditionally, cultural historians have concentrated on the ideas of "great" men and women — artists, scholars, writers, political and religious leaders — thus restricting their definition of culture to what Matthew Arnold termed "the best that has been thought and said." More recently, however, historians have been turning to new kinds of evidence and asking new questions in order to recapture with immediacy different national and local cultures. Influenced by the insights of sociology and anthropology, they have expanded their definition of culture to encompass the thought and expression of all people in society. They seek to unfold the structure of human thought as revealed in "all those things which man has added to nature which would not have existed without man."

To many historians, then, culture has come to mean everything that a society expresses, not only through its writings but through its songs, legends, tools, furniture, architecture, craftwork, even its patterns of behavior. It is with non-written sources, in particular, that historians have been researching the cultural history of groups neglected in traditional accounts. Such sources may be referred to as "cultural artifacts," and include all those objects produced by a society for its own use and information, which can be seen to reflect conditions of thought and relationship common to that society. Because these artifacts have not been produced intentionally as historical records, they often allow both the scholar and the student to see the realities of life in a particular historical period without the self-conscious mediation of its own members.

Teachers throughout New England have experimented with pedagogical methods ranging from audio-visual presentation to on-site inspection of archaeological remains to immerse their students in the cultural environments of unfamiliar historical periods. One assumption behind many of these approaches is that students can more fully appreciate conclusions about past cultures if reached through personal experience of their remains than if taken solely on the authority of teacher or text.

Thus, it seems, the different sources that now concern cultural historians can be joined to effective techniques of teaching, to bring students closer to the ongoing process of historical investigation as well as to the consciousness of past societies.

Building the Statue of Liberty

ARTIFACTS IN THE CLASSROOM

Paul Russell, of Boston College, offers below some general reflections on his experience teaching cultural history.

The use of cultural artifacts in the classroom is hardly new or innovative. The "discovery method" implicit in inductive teaching has been around since the 1950's, but its use has been confined to elementary and a few progressive high schools. Because the nature of the cognitive response that students are required to make is very simple, university educators often reject this technique as unsophisticated. They consider this methodology another manifestation of the audio-technical revolution that has put them out of touch with their students, and thus are "turned off" by the input-output, feedback, A-V syndrome. Yet the new generation of students is accustomed to an environment in which sensual stimuli are of paramount importance. Especially since reading and writing skills are weaker among these students, instructors find it difficult to communicate with them. Students in turn are bored by the endless lectures and lengthy readings characteristic of university classrooms.

One solution is to wire the ivory tower for sound and light! This must be done carefully, to avoid sacrificing the basic structure of the lectures or required readings. As instructors of history we do not have the luxury afforded to art and music historians, whose legitimate role it is to present material for purely esthetic enjoyment. Cultural artifacts must be carefully integrated into the traditional course plan.

To be used effectively in the classroom, cultural artifacts must be presented in ways that are directly linked to the specific teaching objectives of the instructor. Perhaps the most disastrous misuse of such artifacts occurs when instructors decide to "throw in a few slides" for visual appreciation. Unable to grasp the context, students become frustrated or inattentive because they do not understand exactly what they are supposed to learn from the presentation. After a few gallant efforts, the instructor often abandons this approach in disgust.

The choice of artifacts depends to a large degree on class size, since some materials are less suitable for large classes. Here follow some of my successful variations:

Visual Artifacts

Objective: To communicate to students the effect of the industrial revolution on the landscape and attitude of Europeans.

Slides: English cities before and after the rapid growth of industry. Idyllic pastoral scenes compared with early photographs of workers and their families. Eighteenth-century portraits contrasted with nineteenth-century paintings.

Equipment: Two carousel projectors and screen.

Slides can be obtained from various sources, but the easiest and cheapest way to obtain them is to make your own.

Audible Artifacts

Objective: To emphasize the influence and importance of mathematics and balance in the eighteenth century.

Recording: Bach Fuge No. 1 (BWV 1080), **Die Kunst der Fuge**. Record the simple theme first, repeat. Record the next theme. Make two plastic overlays, one for each theme, from the music notation, to indicate exactly how each theme is harmonically balanced. Illustrate the meaning of counterpoint. Play the entire fuge to show possible variations within a limited and defined framework.

Equipment: Overhead projector and screen; Sony TC126 cassette tape recorder with independent stereo speakers.

This requires very little classroom time. More than five minutes of music, however, can be disastrous in classes with more than 40 students.

Documents

Objective: To teach the symbolism and appeal of National Socialism to the German people.

Film: Triumph des Willens (Triumph of the Will), 1934, a propaganda film by Leni Riefenstahl. Use the original German version with simultaneous commentary and translation. Hint: An eighteen-minute marching sequence in the last reel could well be cut down considerably.

Equipment: 16mm sound movie projector and screen.

Although students occasionally grumble about the language of the film, it is an excellent teaching device. It contains all the major symbols used by the Nazis to manipulate the sympathies of the German people.

All these artifacts were used in Western Civilization classes, which draw students from every sector of the university. For many of these students, Western Civilization is their first and last contact with the history of their culture. Used with care, cultural artifacts enhance and deepen this experience.

Finally, I would advise an instructor to limit his or her first attempt to present artifacts to a few minutes. This helps students as well as the instructor to become accustomed to the method. Only if both feel comfortable, aware of common objectives, will it be successful.

P.R.

AMERICAN EXPERIENCE

Judy Spock supervises a program called "American Experience," which uses the cultural resources of Boston to teach American history. Below, she describes her goals and approaches.

The American Experience program is a participatory history course for high school students. Under the aegis of the Education Collaborative for Greater Boston, Metropolitan Education Center, the program is funded by the State Bureau of Equal Educational Opportunity, which seeks to provide positive inter-racial and cross-cultural experiences for young people in Boston.

American Experience brings together students from English High School in Boston and schools in suburban communities for an intensive week of full-day activities. The resulting interchanges are educationally valuable in themselves. For example, we paired a group of Spanish-dominant students from English High, many of whom had been in the country only a year or two, with a group of advanced students of Spanish from Medford High School. Speak-

---

Art and Society

At the School of the Museum of Fine Arts in Boston, Richard Broadman teaches courses on "Art and Society" and "American Art and Culture." Aimed primarily at art students, both courses examine such cultural artifacts as works of high art, illustrations, cartoons, photographs, and dramatic films, along with modern anthropological films and selected readings, to explore the changing role of the artist in different societies and periods. Typical topics: "images of progress" in science fiction; "the American West" on film. Biographies of individual artists, artisans, and entertainers are emphasized, in addition to consideration of their work.

---

ing in both English and Spanish, these young people used whatever they could find in their different backgrounds to communicate and to learn from each other.

Our students explore various themes in the last hundred years of American history, including mobility, immigration, industrialization, the Black experience, and war, with an emphasis on history as reflected in dance, music, and the visual arts. These topics are pursued on site through museum collections, musical performances, mime, media, and discussion. We are not in the business of entertaining students, but try to engage them in their own education within a real urban environment.

When considering the Black experience, for example, students tour the Beacon Hill site of the original Black settlement in Boston, to broaden the context in which they encounter crafts and photography at the Museum of Afro-American History, and music and art at the National Center of Afro-American Artists. And they participate in a history of America through dance with the Movement Lab, Inc., learning the character, ethnic origin, and social significance of different dances ranging from the clog to the hustle.

Boston is a very rich cultural resource, but few suburban youths feel safe in the city and few urban youths know much about it. Since most students have never seen Beacon Hill, Roxbury, or Chinatown, a trip there is an experience in itself. At the beginning of the week we provide buses, but then try to wean them over to the mass transit system. We encourage them to travel in groups. Although occasionally they get lost, we tell them what to do should that happen. They find their way, and grow not only in ideas and information, but in self-awareness, respect for others, and appreciation of our shared human history.

J.S.

LANDSCAPE HISTORY

John R. Stilgoe, of the Department of Visual and Environmental Studies and the Department of Landscape Architecture at Harvard, offers the following commentary on teaching landscape history. In particular, he draws on his experience teaching at Harvard with John Brinckerhoff Jackson, former editor of Landscape. *By way of illustration, Stilgoe has included two of his own photographs, which he uses to explore various themes in American history.*

Landscape history traces the evolution and meaning of the built environment. Just as houses, farms, suburbs, roads, factories, parks, and other artificial modifications of the natural habitat indicate past and present social, religious, economic, and cultural trends and values, the whole man-made landscape reflects every level of design, from the vernacular alterations of barns and backyards to the professional ordering of Spanish settlements and New England towns. Every historical period lives however faintly in the contemporary American landscape.

At Harvard two lecture courses introduce undergraduate and graduate students to landscape analysis. "Studies of the Man-made Envriontion of the United States from 1783 to the Present" begins with the landscape of the Pueblo Indians and concludes with the landscape of franchised commercialization, the strip and shopping center. It covers a wide range of topics chronologically, including the southern influence on American road design, the impact of scientific management and electricity on mills, fac-

tories, and farms, the struggle between engineers and architects for control of urban planning, and the changing landscapes of transportation systems. The spring course, "Studies in the Man-made

---

The course we give is essentially meant for the student who has no prerequisite of any sort except the ability to sit and listen and look. It is devoted to a description of how the American landscape has been formed. This means using as many pictures as possible. The pictures I use are very prosaic. They do not attempt to be art; they show no aspect of the subject that we would fail to see with our eyes. We use whatever is commonplace, that which has no distinction and is everywhere. The things we discuss are fences, roads, barns, churches, schools; all touch upon American social and cultural history.

— John Brinckerhoff Jackson

American small towns are not isolated. Each has its place in a great scheme of fraternal orders, as thousands of edge of town signs show.

Environment of the United States, 1900-1977," is an upper-level analysis of the modern landscape and its perception by the public. It discusses mechanization, national planning, psychological engineering, and other broad themes in terms of such specific landscapes as agribusiness farms, the interstate highway system, New Deal conservation areas, and suburbs of the 1950's.

This year's research seminar concerns American house styles and siting, and is intended to show students what a wealth of material exists on an important but comparatively ignored topic. Analyzing the roles of family relationships, standardized building techniques, recreation and work patterns, and advertising in shaping vernacular dwellings, the seminar features slides, walking tours, and extensive study of original documents.

Making students aware of the man-made landscape is no easy task, for this greatest of all art forms is so extensive that it is seldom consciously observed. It is here that color slides are most important, for they confront students with the landscape as document, and force them to read a new language. The slides edit the landscape and direct attention at specific elements that even the curious traveler is likely to miss. Once aware of any landscape as a landscape (and the Pueblo and Spanish Southwest landscapes are sufficiently different from most students' own to spark interest early in the fall course), students begin questioning others. Eventually they perceive the contemporary landscape not as a haphazard collection of structures and places, but as a planned space where nothing is built without reason.

Secondary source material is hard to obtain. John Brinckerhoff Jackson's *American Space: The Centennial Years: 1865-1876* (1973) is the only solid introduction; *Landscape* and *Environmental Review* are the most useful journals. But the lack of texts is a boon, because students can be started on such theoretical works as Mircea Eliade's *The Sacred and the Profane* (1957) and Yi-Fu Tuan's *Topophilia* (1974), and then encouraged to search old periodicals, travel narratives, local histories, and government publications for descriptions and illustrations of specific landscapes. Old photographs, postcards, silent films, and advertisements are suddenly of more than antiquarian interest. When certain that no secondary literature exists on a particular topic, most students are eager to rummage through primary materials. Their term papers are often original and sometimes significant; several have been published in professional journals.

Sometimes students investigate topics of personal meaning — company towns, three-deckers, urban parks, military posts — but more often they choose landscape elements related to other courses. Economics students will analyze shopping streets, psychology majors will study suburban privacy, and literature concentrators will compare the settings of novels against reconstructed landscapes. Beyond serving as a powerful adjunct to other disciplines, landscape history sharpens students' visual and verbal capacity. To describe a park in terms of a graveyard, or a lawn in terms of a meadow, is to clarify one's sense of place and become aware that the landscape is an intricate artificiality that links past with present and deserves the most careful criticism.

J.R.S.

Nineteenth-century suburbs offered harried city dwellers the chance to organize and define personal space. The picket fence still marks the beginning of the private domain.

Term Paper Suggestions
for Landscape History

The development of the "rumpus room"

The reuse of railroad stations, schools, gas stations

The invention and use of skylights in the dwelling

Nineteenth-century attitudes toward lighting and colored glass in the home

The history of the mansard roof in popular magazines

The history of the prefabricated dwelling

The rise and fall of ceilings (the porch, the basement) in the nineteenth century

The death of the architectural facade

How have barn shapes and forms influenced contemporary architecture?

The development of sports facilities in public parks

The cult of the swimming pool

The experience of "Pullman touring" in the early twentieth century

The location of sporting events in eighteenth-century America

Children's street games — how have they changed?

The development of sport hunting in America

The social effects of the invention of the bicycle

The development of the truck and its impact on the highway

The evolution of a trolley street

The road as seen in Hollywood movies

Reasons behind the selection of certain types of paving in the nineteenth century

The folklore of crossroads (bridges, tunnels, gates)

Farm artifacts in modern suburbia

The origin of "dude" ranching

How has the tractor altered the spatial organization of the American farm?

The history of astrological planting and harvesting beliefs

Uses of the forest in New England since the Revolution

The landscape of company towns

AFRO-AMERICAN FOLK CULTURE

The history of Afro-Americans may be taught as well as investigated through examination of various non-written sources. Here William Ferris of the American and Afro-American Studies programs at Yale University discusses his course on "Black Folklore" and presents some of the materials he has introduced into his classroom.

In this course, I examine the origin and development of Afro-American folk culture from its roots in West African society to the present. A primary assumption of this course is that Black culture is an oral culture, and that an understanding of folk traditions is essential in its study. I focus on the "Black performer" of lore as a community leader who skillfully creates and manipulates oral forms for specific purposes. I call for detailed study of both music and prose narrative, and expect students to utilize film and recorded sources as well as written studies. I place emphasis on the structure and function of folklore forms as they have existed in the Black community. Black folklore has been shaped by the experiences of slavery and rural and urban life, and I have students study it within these contexts.

I divide music into sacred and secular traditions, and trace the development of each. I have my students examine the traditional unaccompanied spiritual and compare it with modern Gospel sound, and discuss such less-known sacred forms as the Dr. Watts hymn and the Sacred Harp Conventions. Secular music begins with the African work chant and its American counterpart, which develops into country blues and later into urban blues. We examine each stage of blues, and explore the relationship between performers and their

music through in-depth studies of Big Bill Broonzy and B.B. King. I invite James Thomas, a Delta blues artist, to perform for the class and discuss his music, and I develop discussions of how blues, soul music, and jazz are related. I have my students study prose narrative forms as they developed from African oral tradition. African trickster tales are traced to the United States, where they evolved in a rural and later an urban environment. I place special emphasis on the protest tale, and on its use of racial stereotypes such as "John" and "Ole Master." Lesser-known obscene forms such as dozens, toasts, and jive are shown to serve a role in secular lore similar to that of the sermon in religious lore.

I have my students study the form and content of the sermon in both rural and urban churches. Using folk sources, we focus on the preacher as a religious spokesman for the community. Since material culture is perhaps the least-studied area of Black folk traditions, we look at examples of sculpture, carving, and quilting to show how they function within the Black community.

Finally, I require each student to present a critique on a book of his choice, and to write a research paper. The paper must involve research in primary sources of folklore, focusing on a specific genre and analyzing its role within the Black community.

W.F.

Othar Turner plays cane fife.

William Ferris

James Thomas sings the blues.

"BLACK FOLKLORE": Class Outline

I. FOLKLORE AND THE SPECTRUM OF BLACK FOLK CULTURE:

Zora Neale Hurston, "My People! My People!," in Alan Dundes, ed., **Mother Wit from the Laughing Barrel** (1973). Eldridge Cleaver, "As Crinkly as Yours," in Dundes, **Mother Wit.** Ralph Ellison, "A Very Stern Discipline," **Harpers Magazine** (March, 1967). Albert Lord, **The Singer of Tales** (1960), pp. 1-138. Alan Dundes, "What Is Folklore?" **The Study of Folklore** (1965). Jan Brunvand, **The Study of American Folklore** (1968), pp. 1-27.

II. ROOTS OF BLACK FOLK CULTURE:

Melville J. Herskovits, **The Myth of the Negro Past** (1941). Sidney Mintz, "Foreword," in Norman E. Whitten, Jr., and John F. Szwed, eds., **Afro- American Anthropology** (1970).

Janheinz Jahn, **Muntu: An Outline of the New African Culture** (1961), pp. 217-239. John W. Work, "Origins," **American Negro Songs** (1940). Lydia Parrish, "African Survivals on the Coast of Georgia," **Slave Songs of the Georgia Sea Islands** (1942). Alan Lomax, ed., **Roots of the Blues**, Atlantic Record 1348, side one, track 7 ("Chevrolet"). John W. Blassingame, **The Slave Community** (1972), pp. 1-40. David Evans, "Black Fife and Drum Music in Mississippi," **Mississippi Folklore Register** (Fall, 1972).

III. THE SLAVE NARRATIVE:

B.A. Botkin, **Lay My Burden Down** (1965). Clifton H. Johnson, Paul Radin, Charles S. Johnson, A.P. Watson, eds., **God Struck Me Dead** (1945), pp. 1-50.

IV. ANIMAL TALES — THE TRICKSTER:

H.C. Brearsley, "The Bad Nigger," in Dundes, **Mother Wit.** C.G. Jung, "On the Psychology of the Trickster Figure," in Paul Radin, ed., **The Trickster** (1956). William Ferris, "Black Prose Narrative in the Mississippi Delta," **Journal of American Folklore** (April-June, 1972). Roger D. Abrahams, "Trickster, The Outrageous Hero," in Tristram Potter Coffin, ed., **Our Living Traditions** (1968). Richard M. Dorson, **American Negro Folktales** (1968). Bernard Wolfe, "Uncle Remus and the Malevolent Rabbit," in Dundes, **Mother Wit.** Duncan Emrich, ed., **Animal Tales in the Gullah Dialect**, Library of Congress Record, AAFS L44-46.

V. STREET CORNER LORE:

Roger D. Abrahams, "Playing the Dozens," in Dundes, **Mother Wit.** William Labov et al., "Toasts," in Dundes, **Mother Wit.** H. Rap Brown, "Street Smarts," in Dundes, **Mother Wit.** Roger D. Abrahams, **Deep Down in the Jungle** (1970). Malcolm X, **The Autobiography of Malcolm X** (1965), pp. 84-125. Eldridge Cleaver, "On Watts," **Soul on Ice** (1968).

VI. THE SERMON:

Bruce Rosenberg, "The Formulaic Quality of Spontaneous Sermons," **Journal of American Folklore** (January-March, 1970). Joseph R. Washington, **Black Religion** (1964), pp. 1-162. Alan Lomax, ed., **Negro Church Music**, Atlantic Record, SD 1351, side one. William Ferris, "The Rose Hill Service," **Mississippi Folklore Register** (Summer, 1972).

VII. WORK CHANTS:

William Ferris, "Railroad Chants: Form and Function," **Mississippi Folklore Register** (Spring, 1970). Lydia Parrish, **Slave Songs of the Georgia Sea Islands**, pp. 197-251. Alan Lomax, ed., **Afro-American Spirituals, Work Songs, and Ballads**, Library of Congress Record, AAFS L3, side B. George Mitchell, **Blow My Blues Away** (1971), pp. 1-58. Alan Lomax, ed., **Roots of the Blues**, Atlantic Record 1348, side two. B.A. Botkin, ed., **Negro Work Songs and Calls**, Library of Congress Record, AAFS L8. **Gravel Springs Fife and Drum** (Film). Bruce Jackson, **Wake Up Dead Man** (1972), pp. 1-4.

VIII. COUNTRY BLUES:

W.C. Handy, **Father of the Blues, An Autobiography** (1941). Leroi Jones, **Blues People: Negro Music in White America** (1963). William Ferris, **Blues From the Delta** (1970). Ralph Ellison, "Blues People," **Shadow and Act** (1964). Alan Lomax, ed., **Afro-American Blues and Game Songs**, Library of Congress Record, AAFS L59. Janheinz Jahn, "Residual African Elements in the Blues," in Dundes, **Mother Wit.**

IX. URBAN BLUES:

"The Migration of Negroes from the South," **Report of the National Advisory Commission on Civil Disorders** (1968), pp. 239-247. Charles Keil, **Urban Blues** (1967). Michael

Haralambos, "Soul Music and Blues," in Whitten and Szwed, eds., **Afro-American Anthropology.** Selected readings from **Blues World, Blues Unlimited,** and **Living Blues.** B.B. King, **Live and Well,** Bluesway Record, BLS 6031. B.B. King, **Indianola Mississippi Seeds,** ABC Record, ABCS-713.

X. SOUL MUSIC AND JAZZ (read any two):

A.X. Nicholas, **The Poetry of Soul** (1971). Phyl Garland, **The Sound of Soul** (1969). Leroi Jones, **Black Music** (1967). Alan Lomax, **Mister Jelly Roll** (1950). André Hodier, **The Worlds of Jazz** (1972). Gunther Schuller, **Early Jazz** (1968).

XI. RELIGIOUS MUSIC:

William Ferris, "The Negro Conversion Experience," **Keystone Folklore Quarterly** (Spring, 1970). John Lovell, Jr., "The Social Implications of the Negro Spiritual," in Dundes, **Mother Wit.** William Francis Allen, Charles Pickard Ware, and Lucy McKim Garrison, "Introduction," **Slave Songs of the United States** (1867). Miles Mark Fisher, "History in the Music of Negroes," **Negro Slave Songs** (1953). B.A. Botkin, ed., **Negro Religious Songs and Services**, Library of Congres Record, AAFS L10. The Staple Singers, **Will the Circle Be Unbroken**, Stax 7508.

XII. MATERIAL CULTURE:

Robert Farris Thompson, "African Influences on the Art of the United States," in Armstead L. Robinson, Craig C. Foster, and Donald A. Ogilvie, eds., **Black Studies in the University** (1969), William Ferris, "James Thomas: Folk Artist," **Studies in the Literary Imagination** (April, 1970). **James Thomas, Delta Artist** (film). Wade Alexander, ed., **God's Greatest Hits** (1970); see illustrations by Sister Morgan. William Ferris, **Mississippi Folk Architecture** (1972).

I helped develop a series of films, records, and slide-tapes in conjunction with my course on folk culture. Many of the materials and songs are from the South, but some are about the music, culture, and religion of Black people in New Haven and northern cities. The film titles are:

Give My Poor Heart Ease: Mississippi Delta Bluesmen
Mississippi Delta Blues
Delta Blues Singer: James "Sonny Ford" Thomas
Gravel Springs Fife and Drum
I Ain't Lying: Folktales from Mississippi
Two Black Churches
Black Delta Religion
Fannie Bell Chapman: Gospel Singer
Made In Mississippi: Black Folk Art and Crafts

There is also a slide-tape, **Got Somethin' To Tell You: Sounds of the Delta Blues,** narrated by B.B. King, and an LP record, **Mississippi Folk Voices.**

Information on these materials plus other bibliographic material can be acquired from The Center for Southern Folklore, 6 Peabody Ave., P.O. Box 4081, Memphis, Tennessee 38104.

W.F.

MATERIAL CULTURE

James Deetz is both a member of the Anthropology Department at Brown University and Assistant Director of Plimoth Plantation. An archaeologist by training, Deetz talks below of his special perspectives on teaching history.

Material culture itself can be styled that segment of man's physical environment which he has modified through his own culturally inherited behavior. Yet we must remember that culture is a mental quality that cannot be touched directly. What we are actually talking about are the products of culture. Among these products are such things as automobiles, Bran Chex boxes, mansions, yoyos, pocket change; all aspects of man's control over the landscape; all manner of human kinesics — for the way we shape our actions is culturally relevant; and language.

There are several important points to be made about the material culture approach. We must adopt the procedures and insights of many disciplines outside traditional history: folklore studies, anthropology, linguistics, archaeology. We must also look to new kinds of evidence, such as that unearthed by the methods of archaeology, and we must look at traditional sources in new ways. Further, and this is very important, we must look at material culture systems as best we can through the eyes of the people who made and used them. If we impose our own categories on the cultural remains of past ages, our understanding will be warped. We must see how people themselves categorized the material culture of which they were a part. This will help us to understand much more how artifacts functioned in real behavioral and cultural contexts.

The principle behind this approach is that artifacts reflect cognitions. Material culture systems represent the minds of the people who put them together. As we study particular artifacts in their real contexts, we can plug into an overall scheme that examines the whole sweep of change in material culture. For instance, one can see changes in worldview in the transition from sprawling, haphazard timberframe houses to symmetrical Georgian mansions, or in the coming of standardized individual place settings for meals, or in the change from spontaneous string band to tightly organized bluegrass music.

What are the advantages of this approach for the historian and teacher? For one thing, the archaeological record is not biased by any grudge that a writer might have had toward his material. I frankly mistrust written records: they are written by people who are often very subjective. No one was carrying any ideological grudge when he threw the garbage out the door. When we dig up that garbage it informs us unintentionally. It is probably the most bias-free evidence we have.

Written records represent only the top five percent of the population. History is habitually elitist: it only talks about people who write, and about the big guys. The common people have left their record behind, but it has to be gotten at in a number of ways other than the analytical methods of traditional historiography.

Thus, if we broaden our approaches, if we look at artifacts — especially the way objects are integrated in systems — as reflective of the way man has looked out upon his world and structured it, much more can be learned than most historians have ever imagined.

J.D.

DIGGING ON CAMPUS

William Turnbaugh teaches archaeology in the Sociology and Anthropology Department at the University of Rhode Island, where he has developed the following program for student investigation of objects from the past.

Field schools traditionally have encouraged and provided the context for much valuable archaeological research. Many young people have found in such programs both stimulating diversion and opportunities to participate directly in legitimate scientific discovery. Not only "routine" sites but many others of unusual importance, however, have become fare for avid student archaeologists during the past decade. There is growing concern among some professionals that the practice of using significant archaeological sites for teaching is overly destructive of the resources of the past. Yet students need on-site experience.

With these points in mind, it is desirable to consider an alternative for introducing neophyte archaeologists to field methods. On-campus excavation is a suitable approach.

Nearly every school takes pride in its beginnings, deriving its identity and spirit in part from recognition of its past and traditions. Most campuses have an area or building closely associated with the establishment or development of the school. Founder's Hall, the first dorm, the old library or chapel — these are heritage centers.

Watson House, the oldest structure at the University of Rhode Island, became the training ground for students enrolled in an archaeological method and theory course. After memos and explanatory phone calls had cleared the way for University approval, fourteen classtime and non-classtime ses-sions in dirt archaeology provided a first set of students with practical instruction that they previously had lacked.

The early stages of this long-range project focused on the area of an "ell" extending from the north side of the house. A walkway and a stone step were uncovered, indicating the position of a doorway that had preceded the nineteenth-century addition. Further excavation showed that a shaded and well-drained spot between the ell and the main building had served the

---

A Victorian Trash Pile

Karin O'Neil and Thomas Smith, teachers at Williston-Northampton School, have their students engage in an archaeological dig as an alternative to "straight" history. They excavate the former site of a coal company where trash of the late Victorian period was used as fill. Students survey the site to form a grid of five-foot squares. Each class that has gone through the process is allowed to dig only in a limited portion of the checkerboard pattern, but this was enough to bring up any number of finds — bottles, toys, kitchen utensils, and the like. Among the technical procedures employed are soil profile analysis and flotation, a process used to recover such fine organic remains as seeds and small bones.

After the dig, students clean the artifacts and color code each item to indicate the exact horizontal and vertical location in which it was found. Each student then researches a particular facet of the site in depth and prepares a report. The choices range widely — tracing druggist's bottles, toys, china patterns — but must reveal to the student the relevance of the dig to history and the complementary relationship of archaeological and traditional historical methods.

Watson family as a dumping area for fuel ash and such diverse household items as broken dishes, food refuse, bricks, and two cast iron toys.

Term projects during the next few years are expected to add increasingly to the scanty historical documentation of Watson House. The reports of each stage of investigation eventually will be compiled into a final publication and become a part of Rhode Island's archaeological record. Just as important, students in coming semesters will be gaining practical field experience in laying out, excavating, recording, interpreting, and backfilling portions of this site on their own campus. Afterwards, in the lab, they will clean, conserve, catalogue, photograph, analyze, and interpret artifacts; they will also construct displays for exhibit at Watson House.

Students can accomplish in part of one semester much of what is attempted in the normal field school curriculum. Further, the Watson House approach could be extended easily into a summer-long project.

W.T.

Adapted from **American Antiquity** (April, 1976).

The Watson House

GRAVEN IMAGES

During the past four years, students in Quincy, Massachusetts, have participated in the restoration of the 337-year-old Hancock Cemetery. Since the cemetery has been used over the centuries as a pasture, a playground, and a training ground for soldiers, many stones have been knocked down or lost. Directed by Richard J. Riley of the Quincy Public Schools and inspired by the model of the Gloucester Community Development Corporation, the project employs students during summer vacations with support from CETA funds, providing them with archaeological techniques to restore existing stones and search for those that are missing (along with other cultural artifacts).

So that the work of these students will be educational and contribute to the life of the community, Riley uses the cemetery as a focus for studying the history of Quincy as a whole. His work plan for the restoration includes an extensive list of historical research projects for students in his classes during the year as well as summer workers. Upon finding the burial plot of an eighteenth-century family, for example, a student may be asked to use archival material to trace its history. Other students use published studies of various New England towns to place the life expectancy of those buried in the cemetery in broader historical context, or study their ethnicity, or even research the importance of changes in land ownership and land use in the area. Riley has observed that his student-workers, some of whom have learning difficulties in school, become almost possessive in their feelings about the cemetery, and proudly give tours to summer visitors.

Riley treats gravestones as artifacts that illustrate the culture of their time.

Comparing gravestone art with lacework, broadsides, wig styles, and architecture, he introduces students to the technology and craft of stone cutting in historical context — what tools were used, how and where the stones were quarried, who the stone cutters were and where they got their designs. Concerning gravestone symbolism, he asks the following questions:

1. Why are there different types of symbolism?

2. How does the symbolism reflect the religious ideology of Puritans and other groups?

3. How does the seriation of styles in Hancock Cemetery compare with other cemeteries? What does comparison of several seriation patterns tell us about cultural change?

4. Does the symbolism used correlate with the economic and social status of the person buried?

5. What is the relationship between gravestone symbolism and other aspects of funerary symbolism and artifacts?

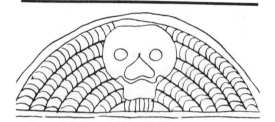

Death's Head

Cherub

Gravestones may reveal changes in religious and cultural attitudes. The spread of the cherub motif in mid-eighteenth-century America, for example, indicates the impact of the intense religious revival that spread through the colonies at that time. Both the Great Awakening and the cherub design, it has been suggested, were "characterized by a newly placed stress on the joys of life after death and resurrection of the dead, rather than the earlier stern emphasis on judgment and mortality." See Edwin Dethlefsen and James Deetz, "Death's Heads, Cherubs, and Willow Trees: Experimental Archaeology in Colonial Cemeteries," **American Antiquity** (April, 1966).

The Gloucester Experiment

Having undertaken a major restoration of historic Bay View Cemetery, the Gloucester Community Development Corporation has published a set of "advisory notes" to aid other communities wishing to preserve or restore old burial grounds. These "notes" supply valuable information on complex legal issues that are pertinent to any restoration. In addition, various participants in the Bay View project have contributed "journals" to assist others in applying the model of the "Gloucester Experiment" elsewhere. They include a monograph by Elsa Martz on "Cemetery Restoration as a High School Course." For further information, write to the Gloucester Community Development Corporation, P.O. Box 15, Gloucester, Massachusetts 01930.

ENGRAVINGS AND THE RENAISSANCE

Alice B. McGinty draws on visual imagery to teach Renaissance history at Bentley College. Below, she offers an example of her approach.

My goal as a historian of early modern Europe is to provide opportunities for my students to discover the characteristics of Western culture as revealed in some of its artifacts. This approach not only makes history more "real" to students but also permits the teacher to get around today's "literacy barrier." It activates students and develops their powers of observation.

One unique artifact I have found helpful in introducing the Renaissance is a series of 24 engravings by Jan Van der Straet called the *Nova Reperta*, or *New Discoveries* (c. 1580-1600). It records the inventions that helped shape the culture of early modern Europe in settings that demonstrate that impact. Van der Straet, a Flemish painter who moved to Florence in 1553, used the copperplate engraving much as television news commentators use today's technical resources to record contemporary events, problems, interests, values, and aspirations. The Frontispiece and Plate One ("America") will illustrate my point.

The one date all students know is 1492 ("Columbus sailed the ocean blue"). "That's news a hundred years later?" they ask when they first see the Frontispiece with its tribute to Columbus. Those who have had Chinese history quickly point out that the Chinese invented gunpowder, silk, the magnet, and printing long before the Europeans. "What's new about the *New Discoveries*?" Here it is helpful to talk about concepts of time: twentieth-century (when "new" is "now") vs. sixteenth-century (when "new" is "not ancient," or any time after the fall of Rome). This leads to a discussion of how

Frontispiece from New Discoveries

people in the Renaissance acquired a more "modern" sense of time, and thus of history. The Frontispiece shows one way Europeans discovered they had invented many things unknown to the Ancients: stirrups, striking clocks, gunpowder, cannon, the compass, distillation, printing. The biggest discovery of all was America (three continents and the Pacific Ocean). What Ancient could match that? The allegorical images at the top corners of the Frontispiece reflect the feeling Renaissance men had that they

lived in a new time. An American Amazon carrying a uroborus — a symbol of time and wisdom — enters the scene; Ancient Wisdom exits right.

The composition of the Frontispiece raises many questions. Why does the cannon dominate it? (Like the press, stirrups, clock, compass, and engraving, it shows Europe's lead in metallurgy.) The teacher quotes contemporary accounts of how American Indians reacted to cannon fire and the sight of men on horses, and how Europeans reacted to their discovery that the Americans lacked iron weapons (and needles, striking clocks, presses, compasses). This leads to a discussion of the place of technology in our culture, then and now, and the relation of material to non-material culture. Students then seem more appreciative of the great skill Cellini displays in the bust of Bindo Altovitti — which they see on a field trip to the Gardner Museum.

Plate 1 ("America") recreates Vespucci's landfall in South America. Van der Straet assembles in one image, from the earliest printed accounts of the discoveries, those elements that Europeans found shocking in America one hundred years after Columbus: nudity, Amazons, cannibals, bizarre animals (anteater, sloth, tapir, opossum), and exotic plants (pineapple). This image serves well as an example of Burckhardt's classic definition of the Renaissance: the discovery of the world, of man, and of nature. It also shows how a foreign craftsman from Bruges could become a historian in late sixteenth-century Florence. This leads into a discussion of the nature of Florentine society (its degree of mobility), and of the Renaissance in general.

The *New Discoveries* is effective in teaching Renaissance history because it is visual — the current perceptual mode of our students. It is sufficiently strange to create a sense of distance between the sixteenth and the twentieth centuries; yet it exhibits enduring traits of Western culture.

A.B.M.

Art and Its Context

Anne H. Van Buren, of the Art History Department at Tufts University, comments below from the perspective of an art historian on the uses of art in teaching history.

Most of the art that has survived is elitist. The further back one goes the more one is forced to rely on what has been produced by a small segment of society. I share a concern for the silent masses of people who have lived and died throughout history, but the priority of art historians is to understand products of art in the same way they were understood in their own time.

The work of Albrecht Durer, for example, is particularly well suited to study of the period in which it was made. Durer exploited the medium of prints to an unprecedented degree, and made a commercial success of it. Because his powerful visual images were relatively cheap, they reached the mass of people, who had hardly ever seen such pictures before.

Any teacher who wishes to use art must first get to know very well the works of art characteristic of a particular time. It is important that historians not simply illustrate their subjects, but learn to analyze pictures to bring out the complex relationships of art to the society that produces it. Here, perhaps, the interests of the general historian and the specialist in art history converge.

A.H.V.B.

"America" from New Discoveries

IMAGES AND INSIGHT

Rudi Lindner, who has taught at Tufts University and is now at the University of Michigan, comments below on his experience using visual images in courses on Medieval and Near Eastern history.

In the history classroom art allows neat, short proofs of three propositions: civilizations have style; styles (unspoken conceptions of taste) vary among cultures; certain (perhaps all) conclusions that historians reach in their work are recognized before they are demonstrated.

Students now are very familiar with color television. Just any old cultural artifact does not suffice to awaken Trekkies. Thus the teacher must use slides to make points and to suggest that students observe as well as see — and, by extension, read with the mind's eye as well. In short, a slide does not adorn a lecture. If so, it is unnecessary, like a joke or a reference to office hours. The slide must make a point, or destroy an assumption. It has to be well-chosen.

Art in a Medieval European history course, for instance, can meet all these requirements very effectively. Students digest Gregory of Tours or Beowulf and conjure up visions of barbarians — better, of an international standard barbarian. This image draws upon a heavy-handed reading of the sources (or of a boring schematic textbook in the manner of those two great historians, Messrs. Barnes and Noble) and creates a dreary pattern. A slide of the purse clasp in the Sutton Hoo burial breaks the pattern and leads students to the realization that lack of public gentility need not preclude artistic achievement. Breaking re-ceived patterns is important if we are helping people to think, not just to memorize.

By extension, slides can be used for classical or traditional Near Eastern history. One can present, for example, the view toward Hagia Sophia from the Karye Camii. This demonstrates the power and pretension of sixth-century Rome, the largest structure in the Western world for eight centuries hulking on the horizon. New Yorkers will appreciate what the skyline must have meant for Byzantine political ideology, the holy Godzilla of late Antiquity protecting the city. One can then present the view toward the Karye Camii from Hagia Sophia. Of course the Karye Camii is too small to be recognized. The two slides work to display the fall of Byzantium — the lack of construction capital in the fourteenth century, and a reminder of the olden days, a contrast that explains the fatalism and vapors of the Palaeologan authors.

Slides can also be used in modern Near Eastern courses, and not simply to show the rather obvious differences between a camel in Damascus and a camel in Konya. In particular, illustrations help students understand the strains that foreign influence brought to the area. For us, "modern" is a good word, and the notion of a "present shock" is hard to transmit in a lecture. I found good slides (at left) in the illustrations to Mustafa Cezar's book *Osman Hamdi Bey ve sanatta Batiya acilis* (1971). Here, a highly cultured Ottoman with Western training from Oxford clashes with his Eastern subjects. One can see Osman Hamdi Bey in his Oxford regalia, and at the same time a contemporary painting depicting a young woman squating sacrilegiously on a sacred Koran stand, having scattered the scholarship of ages across the floor. The juxtaposition and clash, and what it can lead to, becomes clear to students.

R.L.

Osman Hamdi Bey

Young woman on Koran stand

IDEOGRAPHS AS CULTURAL DOCUMENTS

In their course on "Modern World Societies," social studies teachers at Newton North High School in Newton, Massachusetts, examine modernization, rural change, and urbanization in terms of cultural artifacts that illustrate day-to-day life in seven nations. Below, one of these teachers, Richard Reid, explains their approach.

We focus on developing a conceptual framework for understanding history, especially the history of countries other than our own. By so doing, we hope students will discover similarities and dissimilarities of experience between these countries and the United States and place our history within a larger global context. Cultures evolve continually, but the events recorded in conventional history are too isolated and unusual to register this important process. We stress the dynamics of cultural change because this is a kind of history that is otherwise apt to go unnoticed, or be interpreted by students only within the cultural context familiar to them — the here and now. Our course attempts to broaden and deepen their view of society.

I would like to illustrate this general statement of purpose with a particular class that we have adapted from the Japanese workshop provided through the Harvard East Asian Education Project at Boston's Children's Museum. To many of our students, the characters of the Japanese writing system represent random doodlings typical of a most peculiar people. In this exercise we try to show how symbols evolved from pictographs, and how they illuminate the history of Japanese culture.

In a previous class students have been given another exercise in which they are divided into small groups and asked to devise symbols to represent such standard words as fire, woman, running, water, etc. They usually enjoy this, but at first fail to see its relevance to our exercise on the evolution of Japanese characters. We try to show how and why in Japanese history certain characters have changed, constantly becoming more abstract and stylized.

These materials are taken from a book used by Japanese school children, from which we hope our students will gain some sense of closeness to Japanese students as well as understand something of the logic of their system, and of their interest in the precise, the spare, and the terse. From this and similar exercises with Chinese characters, we also hope our students can learn something about the evolution of langauge. Finally, since Japanese writing is Chinese in origin and the Western alphabet is also in use in Japan, our class is designed to teach students something about the processes of acculturation and assimilation.

R.R.

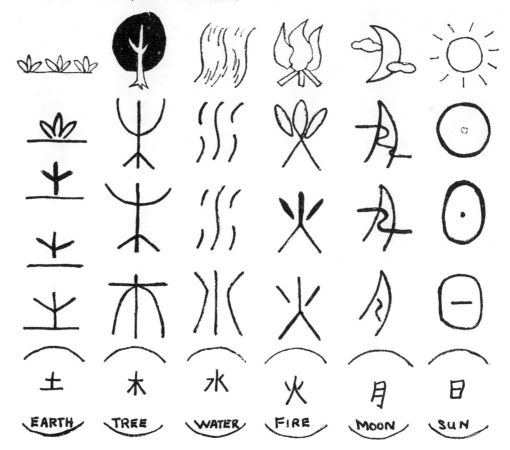

Ideographs supplied by Karen Weisel, Children's Museum

HARD TIMES IN PHOTO AND FILM

In his course on "American Culture in Depression and War," Barry O'Connell of Amherst College relies heavily on visual evidence from both film and photographic sources. On the opposite page, O'Connell explains his objectives and strategies in teaching with such materials. Below, he discusses more specifically the potential of photography as a source for teaching the history of the Depression.

Photographs are especially powerful and tantalizing images of the past because of their immediacy. More even than the movies, photography has given us and those who lived through the Depression most of our images of the decade. When we think of eroded soil and dust storms, suffering farmers, starving children, people in despair, we are probably remembering a photograph taken by a Farm Security Administration (FSA) photographer as much as we are approaching the dominant economic and social realities of the 1930's.

Below is a list of collections of photographs by the principal photographers of the period. Included are some more specialized, private images of the decade by photographers either less well-known than Lange or Evans or Bourke-White or less commonly associated in the mind's eye with the Depression.

For Walker Evans see **American Photographs** (1938); **Let Us Now Praise Famous Men** (consult both 1941 and 1961 editions, photos are different); **Many Are Called** (1966); **Message from the Interior** (1966); **Walker Evans** (1971); and **Walker Evans: Photographs from the FSA** (1973).

For Dorothea Lange, **An American Exodus** (1939); **American Country Woman** (1967); and **Dorothea Lange** (1966).

There is no collection devoted exclusively to Russell Lee, but F. Roy Stryker, ed., **In This Proud Land** (1973), has a generous selection of his work.

For Ben Shahn, **Ben Shahn, Photographer** (1973) and **The Photographic Eye of Ben Shahn** (1975).

For Margaret Bourke-White, see Bourke-White and Erskine Caldwell, **You Have Seen Their Faces** (1937), her major photo-essay of the 1930's; the issues of **Life** (begins publishing in 1936); and the photographs from the 1930's and 1940's in **The Photographs of Bourke-White** (1972).

For Berenice Abbott, **Changing New York** (1939); and **Photographs** (1970).

For Paul Strand, **Paul Strand, 1915-1945** (1945); **Paul Strand, a Retrospective**, volume 1 (1972); and **Time in New England** (1950).

For Doris Ulman, **Appalachian Photographs** (1971) and **The Darkness and the Light** (1974).

Robert Capa, **Death in the Making** (1936), presents his remarkable pictures of the Spanish Civil War. Lewis Hine, **Men at Work** (1932), has unforgettable pictures of high steel construction in Manhattan. Eudora Welty, **One Time, One Place** (1971), presents some extraordinary snapshots of Mississippi during the Depression. J. McManigal, **Farm Town: A Memoir of the Thirties** (1974), takes on interest when compared to photographs of rural life in the Dperession by Lange, Lee, and Shahn. Two good collections of the work of all the Farm Security Administration photographers (including otherwise unavailable photographs by major photographers) are **In This Proud Land** and Arthur Rothstein et al., eds., **A Vision Shared** (1970).

F. Jack Hurley, **Portrait of a Decade** (1972); Beaumont Newhall, **The History of Photography** (1971); William Stott, **Documentary Expression and Thirties America** (1973), and John Szarkowski, **Looking at Photographs** (1973), are excellent historical and critical accounts of many of these photographers and their work.

The Farm Security Administration photographs imposed themselves on the times and on subsequent generations as the truest representations of what the Depression was like. Yet the people who figured most in these photographs could have been revealed to the nation in the 1920's. The plight of tenant farmers, coal miners, agricultural laborers, and small farmers in the 1920's was nearly as bad as during the Depression. These people were invisible during a time we still persist in remembering as the Jazz Age, the great, glittering, prosperous, roaring 1920's. Even the simplest historical generalization the FSA photographs might seem unquestionably to support — the extent and seriousness of poverty among the common people of America — cannot be sustained. The photographs instead raise quite another kind of historical question. What changed in American society that not only made these hitherto excluded people suddenly visible, but also made them the most real images of what the Depression was all about? The question belongs more in the province of cultural and intellectual history than to social history. The answers to it reveal much more about the makers and consumers of these photographic images than the photographs reliably reveal of their subjects.

B.O'C.

American Culture in Depression and War

Literature, photography, and film stand in no clear or self-evident relationship to the culture of a particular time and place. Artists obviously "belong" to a national culture in one sense, but the nature of their belonging differs from artist to artist and from one historical period to another. The 1930's and 1940's were two decades of intense political and social crisis in Western culture. This crisis affected many artists very directly: writers self-consciously sought to make sense of the crisis in their writing; many who had published before the beginning of the Great Depression dramatically altered not only the subject of their work but also its form. The impact of the events of these decades on film-makers was no less severe than on writers but it was far less directly reflected than in much of the writing of the period. Few films concerned themselves directly with the Depression and yet the mark of the greatest economic crisis in American history is on nearly every film produced during the 1930's. Photographers — perhaps virtually driven to it by the nature of their medium — portrayed the decade the most literally of all these artists.

In "American Culture in Depression and War," I examine artists' consciousness of

Edwin Locke

A film should be interpreted as expressive, at least in part, of the vision of the person behind the camera.

these two decades as it is reflected in their work: what did they choose as images for what they experienced and imagined and how do their choices reveal themselves and some aspects of the nation's cultural life? In offering this course I have several purposes in mind. One is negative. I want the students to understand by trying to work with a wide range of literary, historical, and artistic material how complicated it is to write something I call cultural history. I want also to bring them to be able to question in a rather sophisticated way any generalization about the period. Finally, I hope to teach them something about how to interpret not only literary and conventional historical documents but also visual artifacts.

The first task is to teach students something about interpreting films. I do very little with the technical side of filmmaking, since I have found that students would rather discuss "montage," etc., than face the harder task of interpreting the film before them. It is a little like what some students in a poetry class will do with "symbols" to avoid the poem itself. Essentially, I approach the film as a kind of text — visual, auditory, and verbal — and try to get the students to talk first about their responses to the film.

Sometimes I am able in this way to help

them find some ground for speculating about the various ways an audience in the 1930's might have responded to a particular film. Lectures and readings suggest some of the possible different kinds of audiences at the time. Furthermore, although we cannot readily assume what was happening among a variety of audiences on the basis of the film evidence, we can discover something about who the filmmakers thought was "out there" and how they might be reached. With the scanty evidence we have about film attendance, we can then speculate about the audience in terms of which films succeeded and which failed.

The photographs are used in similar ways. I try to give students a sense of how drastically the style of photography changed with the onset of the Depression, with the advent of documentary photography. Instead of making a series of relatively straightforward factual statements about people's lives during the Depression, however, the photographs raise the same kinds of questions as the films. Why was a particular kind of subject chosen? How was it seen? And why was it imaged in the way it was? Superficially the subjects were the same: tenant farmers, migrants, cotton farmers, the people of the plains. But the very similarity in their subject matter makes dramatically clear how differently each photographer conceived his task. Each had a different aesthetic. These photographers were as much involved in constructing an interpretation of the world as the filmmakers — and the novelists — of the period.

B. O'C.

THE CRISIS OF THE GREAT DEPRESSION

How may film be considered source material for history? What can film tell students that cannot be learned from other kinds of evidence? At Harvard University a film series and undergraduate seminar have explored the social consequences of the Great Depression in Britain and America, as registered on film. Here is the program of the series:

SESSION 1: LEISURE

What patterns of leisure activity emerged in reponse to a decade of economic crisis? *Today We Live* (1937), a Paul Rotha production, recorded and promoted British efforts to revive traditional modes of group recreation. *How to Take a Vacation* (1941), a low-budget Robert Benchley one-reeler, satirized the "masculine" American image of a sportsman's holiday. *Easy Living* (1937), which presented Jean Arthur in a Preston Sturges screenplay, was one of the most successful of the "goofy comedies" that Hollywood was able to sell to Depression audiences. Is it plausible to characterize the film as an appeal to "white-collar escapism"?

SESSION 2: TECHNOLOGY

The Depression called into question predictions that the increased productivity of new technologies would bring abundance and happiness. Filmmakers responded in different ways. Robert Flaherty and John Grierson extolled the survival of craftsmanship in *Industrial Britain* (1933), while Albert Cavalcanti's *Men in Danger* (1939) stressed the physical and psychological hazards of work in British mines and factories. Among American films, Willard Van Dyke's controversial *Valley Town* (1940) portrayed the shattering effects of technological unemployment; by contrast, Walter Niebuhr's *Machine: Master or Slave?* (1941) suggested that the threat to jobs and well-being was only temporary.

SESSION 3: THE URBAN POOR

Housing and health care for the urban poor had long been of concern to middle-class social reformers. During the Depression filmmakers began to encourage slum dwellers to tell their own story. *Housing Problems* (1935), co-directed by Sir Arthur Elton, was a rough, journalistic series of unrehearsed interviews in South London. *A Place to Live* (1941) was an attempt by the Philadelphia Housing Authority to translate their statistics into a human document. In *The Fight for Life* (1940), the first feature film made by the U.S. government, Pare Lorentz integrated professional actors with the staff and patients of a maternity clinic in a Chicago slum. What explains the failure of the U.S. Film Service to follow through on this early experiment?

SESSION 4: SOCIAL SERVICES

As debate over the nature and extent of government services intensified, American and British officialdom introduced still another service — the propaganda film — to explain their point of view. *Night Mail* (1936) was a General Post Office production, narrated by W.H. Auden. In *The River* (1938) Pare Lorentz combined lyrical, Whitmanesque evocation of rural America with publicity for the TVA. *The Power and the Land* (1940), directed by Joris Ivens, with commentary by Stephen Vincent Benet, was produced by the U.S. Department of Agriculture to show the impact of rural electrification on farm life.

SESSION 5: AMERICAN WORKERS

Labor films of the 1930's not only documented the advances of the labor movement but also served as organizing tools. *Millions of Us* (1936) and *People of the Cumberland* (1937) are two examples of shorts by radical filmmakers working outside the commercial movie industry. Within the industry, Paramount executives sought to suppress their newsreel of the *Memorial Day Massacre* (1937), because they felt it was inflammatory. Perhaps the most ambitious effort to use film as both a document and an organizing device was *United Action Means Victory* (1940), a forty-minute production of the United Auto Workers' Film Department celebrating the 1939 GM tool and die strike.

SESSION 6: BRITISH WORKERS

The Stars Look Down (1940), an early Carol Reed feature starring Michael Redgrave and Margaret Lockwood, based on a novel by A.J. Cronin, depicted labor problems in the British coal mining industry with unusual realism and evenhanded judgment. MGM brought the film to the U.S., then held it in its vault for over a year before releasing it with the suggestion that exhibitors try to attract customers by drawing "American parallels" in their advertising. Apparently, this and other strategies to promote the film in the U.S. proved ineffective. Why?

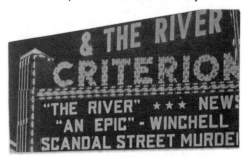

TEACHING WITH POPULAR AMERICAN FILMS

When using Hollywood films in a history course, it is important to help students place them in specific historical context. Students should be encouraged to think about who wrote, produced, directed, and advertised a particular film, and how all these people were influenced both by their personal backgrounds and by the times in which they were working. One way to encourage historical thinking about popular films is to provide supporting documents. Film reviews are obvious and easily available sources, as are film advertisements. Such trade publications as *Variety* and *Motion Picture Herald* provide miscellaneous information concerning film attendance as well as advertising campaigns. The New York Public Library at Lincoln Center maintains convenient files on particular films, along with a microfilm collection of "press books" — advertising manuals supplied by Hollywood distributors to theater owners. Another set of film files is located at the Museum of Modern Art in New York.

The literature on film is so vast as to defy brief summary. Robert Sklar's **Movie-Made America** (1975) and Garth Jowett's **Film: The Democratic Art** (1976) are two useful surveys of the social and cultural history of Hollywood; Lewis Jacobs's **The Rise of the American Film** (1939) is also worth consulting. On the documentary film, see Forsyth Hardy, ed., **Grierson on Documentary** (1946); Lewis Jacobs, **The Documentary Tradition** (1971); and Richard Barsam, **Nonfiction Film** (1973).

Among the many books on film theory and criticism, teachers might begin with André Bazin, **What is Cinema?** (1968); Ralph Stephenson and Jean Debrix, **The Cinema as Art** (1968); or Gerald Mast and Marshall Cohen, eds., **Film Theory and Criticism** (1974). Collections of film criticism, such as **Agee on Film** (1964), may also be useful, along with such specific studies as Molly Haskell's **From Reverence to Rape** (1974) on women, and Daniel Leab's **From Sambo to Superspade** (1975) on Blacks.

Film & History and its British counterpart **University Vision** are journals that report developments in both scholarship and teaching.

The following document is taken from a column in *Motion Picture Herald* called "Selling Points on the New Product." The column suggests how theater exhibitors might best promote and advertise "Talk of the Town." This was a 1942 comedy with a socio-political message, directed by George Stevens and starring Cary Grant, Ronald Colman, and Jean Arthur. In conjunction with a showing of the film, students might consider why Columbia's advertising campaign was so apparently frivolous. What does this reveal about American popular culture in the era of World War II?

TALK OF THE TOWN (Columbia): A teaser campaign is suggested by the title of this picture. A teaser idea is to have a film can beribboned and placed on a pedestal in the lobby with a sign reading "When this is opened it will be the 'Talk of the Town'." A "hush" poster has been prepared, copy on which says, "Don't let **America's** secrets become the Talk of the Town". This poster also has illustrations of the three stars and room for theatre imprint. A venetian blind could be installed in an empty store window; on one side copy could read, "It's the Talk of the Town," and on the other side the playdates. There's a four-day contest suggested which sells the stars and the director; the idea is to have newspaper readers state the name of the picture which brought fame to each of the stars, given an illustration to help. Including the director makes the contest sufficiently difficult to be intriguing. There are a number of stills which are available for local exploitation purposes. One of Jean Arthur using the telephone might be placed in the telephone company's business office. Another, in which she is seen in Ronald Colman's pajamas, could be used in men's store windows with emphasis on the fact that, while these particular ones don't fit Miss Arthur, the store has pajamas to fit anyone. There's a still of Cary Grant busy in the kitchen which can be used to promote kitchenware. The fact that borscht figures prominently in the picture can be used to get space on the woman's page to list a recipe (given in the pressbook). A cooperative page with merchants each calling their wares "The Talk of the Town" seems feasible. Neither Ronald Colman nor Cary Grant has ever played in a picture in which they did not win the girl; obviously this is a first for Colman. Newspaper or program readers can state whether they think Jean Arthur made a wise choice, with prizes for the best answer. In the picture Jean Arthur plays the role of a secretary, suggesting the possibility that local secretaries can be circularized by means of a herald written in shorthand — Gregg on one side and Pittman on the other. The title phrase can be used by the newspaper as a peg on which to hang photos of past events which were the talk of the town in bygone days.

MODERN WAR AND ITS IMAGES

Many teachers in the New England region have built history courses around film. Below, Eugene P.A. Schleh, of the University of Maine at Portland-Gorham, describes his approach to the medium.

My course, "Modern War and its Images," attempted to provide a framework within which students could meet their individual interests. It was to offer a novel approach to military history, a focus for important philosophical questions, a continuing study of mass-media philosophy, or an examination of film technique. In fact, more than half of the students enrolled were history majors, and concern with detailed military-political history tended to dominate most discussions. Smaller numbers of students, however, were enrolled from a wide range of disciplines — including criminal justice, nursing, business, and education.

An open letter to the entire University elicited over three dozen guest discussants. Chaplains, current professional servicemen, infantry and air force veterans, and peace workers joined philosophers, literature specialists, nurses, lawyers, and historians.

At the beginning of the course students were given common responsibilities. Each was to see the films scheduled, and to submit a brief reaction paper every Friday afternoon. I then read these to identify subjects worth pursuing in the seminar scheduled for the beginning of the following week. Each student also selected one of the scheduled films as the basis for a major paper, which was to cover its setting, factual accuracy, critical reception, and literary source. Beyond this common core, each paper was to be developed in accordance with the student's interests. At the appropriate seminar meeting, the student would join guests in leading discussion of topics emerging from the film.

As a veteran of pre-television neighborhood theaters, where one criterion for judging a show was "the more the better," I had to concede gradually that the big double-feature is finished, at least when sandwiched into a heavy student course load. It seems better to prune out personal favorites than to tax student interest through excessive length or presentation of an overwhelming range of subjects.

Guest discussants also proved a mixed blessing. They did stir some of the most provocative and informative discussions. In addition, I remain convinced that it is useful for students to obtain a new perspective from individuals previously considered only in terms of such sterile labels as "English Instructor," or "University Vice-President." Too often, however, guests tended quite unintentionally to intimidate both student discussion leaders and the class as a whole. This was particularly true when several guests attended the same seminar.

In general, the course relied too heavily on the stimulating effect of film. Some students could be counted on to leave a film showing and seek out further information about the subject, but too often requests were made for more specific guidance and for more assigned readings. Thus, in my revised course plan, student assignments were rearranged to rest more heavily on common readings; class time still provided for student innovation in the subject matter. With more extensive readings for background, students met together in small groups immediately following a film showing. These discussions, without fixed time limits, replaced the weekly reaction papers in identifying key subjects for the following week's seminar.

The course retained its central focus on feature films, but strong favorable reaction to documentaries led to greater use of this genre, including two documentaries produced for television rather than for theater audiences. The course syllabus, revised, was as follows:

World War I in Retrospect: **All Quiet on the Western Front** (1930). **Paths of Glory** (1957).
Reactions to Civil War in Ireland and Spain: **The Informer** (1935), **Suffer the Little Children** (1969), **Blockade** (1938).
Morale in the Face of Defeat: **December 7, 1941** (1956), **Wake Island** (1942).
Instant Propaganda: **Hangmen Also Die** (1943).
Air War From Three Views: **The Memphis Belle** (1946), **Target for Tonight** (1941), **Luftwaffe** (1958).

Combat on the Ground: **The Story of G.I. Joe** (1945), **The Battle of San Pietro** (1945).
Liberation: **Open City** (1946), **The Liberation of Paris** (1944).
Demobilization and Reabsorption: **The Best Years of Our Lives** (1946).
Re-evaluation: **The Camps of the Dead** (1945), **Judgment at Nuremburg** (1961).
The P.O.W.: **The Great Escape** (1963).
Contemporary War: **The Anderson Platoon** (1967).

Books for the course were: Hanson W. Baldwin, **World War I: An Outline History** (1962); Martha B. Hoyle, **A World in Flames** (1970); E.R. Remarque, **All Quiet on the Western Front** (1930); Ernest Hemingway, **The Fifth Column and Four Stories of the Spanish Civil War** (1972); Norman Mailer, **The Naked and the Dead** (1948); Pierre Bouille, **The Bridge Over the River Kwai** (1954); Ernie Pyle, **Here Is Your War** (1943); and Time Magazine Editors' **Time Capsule, 1942** (1967).

E.P.A.S.

Adapted from **Film & History** (September, 1973)

WOMEN IN AMERICAN FILM

Mary Blewett, of the University of Lowell, draws on popular films in teaching the history of American women.

Films are one of the great storehouses of society's steroetypes about women. There are two useful ways to handle films about women. You can illustrate the consistent use of degrading sex stereotypes by the film industry, despite superficial changes in style and mood. A better approach is to mix films that portray women as victims with examples of films showing women in strong, aggressive roles. Most films have something to say about sex roles in society, but certain films convey a total view of how a culture limits women's lives.

One film that does this well, and does it with great style and character, is D.W. Griffith's *Way Down East* (1920), which was made the same year as the passage of the women's suffrage amendment and celebrates the nineteenth-century cult of true womanhood. An immensely popular film in the early 1920's, *Way Down East* is a splendid example of the way traditional ideas about women were reenforced in the public by the new film media.

Silent films of the 1920's are a good source of woman-as-victim films. There is the shocking masochism of Yasmin, the dancing girl (Vilma Banky), set against the "macho" brutality of Valentino in *The Son of the Sheik* (1927). The theme of woman-as-devil is also explored in the silents. Inevitably the evil woman is marked by overt and aggressive sexuality. A good example of this is Greta Garbo in *The Flesh and the Devil* (1927), in which she plays both title roles. But to portray women as sexually aggressive was dangerous for Hollywood if these women failed to be suitably punished at the conclusion. Mae West's earthy performances in a series of films ending with

She Done Him Wrong (1933) brought public pressure that forced Hollywood to reactivate the Production Code.

A fascinating but horrendous attack on the nature of women written by a woman is Clare Booth Luce's play and filmscript *The Women* (1939). The plot revolves around an all-female cast whose absorbing passion is intense competition with each other over the possession of off-screen husbands. The theme of women as threatening competitors is also explored in *A Letter to Three Wives* (1949), set in the upper class suburbs of Connecticut.

Another film of the late 1940's takes the theme of competition, but uses it positively to show women as successful professionals. *Adam's Rib* (1949) portrays a woman lawyer (Katherine Hepburn) locked in battle with her husband (Spencer Tracy), a prosecuting attorney, over an attempted murder case. It is clear that Hepburn feels enormous anxiety over beating Tracy, and the effect of it nearly destroys their relationship.

In *Born Yesterday* (1950), Judy Holliday plays the dimwit blonde mistress of a tough guy (Broderick Crawford); but when she meets liberal journalist William Holden, she discovers that she has a brain. Under Holden's tutelage, she rebels against Crawford's brutal control of her, but ends up unliberated in Holden's arms.

Finally, the films of the 1960's and 1970's offer many choices for a women's history course, including both commercial films and films produced and directed by feminists. *The Pumpkin Eater* (1965), with a Harold Pinter screenplay featuring Anne Bancroft, is a difficult and disturbing look at a London housewife trapped by her childbearing role. *Rachel, Rachel* (1969), with Joanne Woodward, sympathetically portrays the awakening of a thirtyish schoolteacher from childish dependence and asexuality. *Janie's Janie* (1972), distributed by feminist Odeon Films (N.Y.C.), focuses on a white New Jersey welfare mother trying to redefine herself as her own person and deal with her responsibilities.

M.B.

Adapted from **Film & History** (December, 1974).

Guide to Film Ordering

A wide range of university and commercial distributors supply films for classroom use. In general, university rental rates are considerably lower than those of commercial companies, but their service is often less reliable and their film prints tend to be of poorer quality.

While universities distribute some feature films, they emphasize educational films and documentaries. Their catalogues are usually mammoth compendiums of whatever has come their way. Among the largest and most useful university film distributors are Boston University and Syracuse University. The University of Illinois has a special catalogue of history films.

For most feature films, it is necessary to turn to commercial distributors. Although rental prices of a distributor will vary from film to film, Budget Films (Los Angeles), Audio-Brandon Films (Mount Vernon, N.Y.), and Wholesome Film Center (Boston) are reliable, inexpensive companies.

It is a good idea to build up your own library of film catalogues, since they supply useful information about the films as well as their rental prices. Distributors will send you their catalogues for free or a small fee. To find out where a particular film is available for rental, one can consult one of the general directories owned by most audio-visual centers.

MASS CULTURE AND COUNTRY MUSIC

Below, Ronald Story of Clark University explains how he makes use of advertisements and popular music in his teaching, to get at central issues of American social and cultural history.

WE CAN'T TALK

Without showing the condition of our *Teeth*. Every laugh exposes them. In order not to be ashamed of them be sure to cleanse them every day with Fragrant *SOZODONT*, and they will be kept white and spotless. The regular use of this peerless dentrifice prevents and arrests dental decay, and the gums are kept healthy and hard. *SOZODONT* removes every impurity that adheres to the teeth, and prevents the formation of Tartar, that great enemy of the teeth. Impure Breath is completely neutralized by the anti-acid and disinfectant properties of *SOZODONT*.

SOLD BY ALL DRUGGISTS.

I use a set of 60 transparencies of advertisements from nineteenth-century mass-circulation magazines.

The first 30 are from the period 1865-1875 and illustrate (a) the development of a primitive but energetic advertising industry which served to enlarge the market for mass-produced commodities and provide revenues for the periodicals; and (b) the emergence of a middle class with anxieties about career success, health, residential and grooming proprieties, and marriage and family life.

The second 30 are from the period 1890-1900 and illustrate (a) the development of a sophisticated advertising profession suggestive of the growth of urban service industries and the specialization of urban labor; and (b) the emergence of a middle class anxious to emulate the national upper class by purchasing the commodities of now familiar industrial giants.

These advertisements reflect the transition from a crude, individualistic, laissez-faire capitalist society with one set of anxieties to a more urbane, stratified, monopolistic society with a somewhat different set of anxieties.

I also use a set of recordings of "hillbilly" or "country and western" music illustrating the migration of rural white southerners to industry and city during the twentieth century. The music is discussed in terms of its lyrical content, the character of its sound, and its changing mode of production and consumption, in order to suggest the shifting circumstances, values, and dilemmas of a somewhat neglected (being neither Black nor immigrant) but still important and in some cases representative element of the working class.

Examples are furnished in the following playlist, which indicates the basic themes I develop and provides information as to performer and label.

R.S.

The Rural Tradition, 1800-1900

The Balladeer

"The War Is A-Raging," Polly Joines, North Carolina (Folkways)
"Most Fair Beauty Bright," Jean Ritchie, Kentucky, with dulcimer (Folkways)
"Barbry Allen," Granny Porter, Virginia, with fiddle (Folkways)
"Ten Thousand Miles," Ruby Vass, Virginia, with guitar (Folkways)
"Waggoner's Lad," Buell Kazee, Kentucky, with banjo (Folkways)

The Ensemble

"Black Eyed Susan," Nestor & Edmonds, Tennessee (RCA)
"Mississippi Sawyer," The Mainer Family, North Carolina (Arhoolie)
"Run Mountain," The Mainer Family
"Amazing Grace," Old Regular Baptist Church, Kentucky (Folkways)
"Precious Memories," Jean Ritchie
"An Empty Mansion," The Stanley Brothers, Virginia (Rimrock)
"This World Is Not My Home," The Stanley Brothers
"I'll Meet You In the Morning," The Stanley Brothers

N.B.CO BUTTER THIN

AMERICA'S MOST POPULAR BISCUIT

"Ground Hog," The Watson Family, North
   Carolina (Folkways)
"Darlin' Cory," The Watson Family
"Down the Road," The Watson Family

The Conservative Tradition

"You Must Unload," The Reed Family,
   West Virginia (Rounder)
"Going to Georgia," Mainer & Morris, North
   Carolina (RCA)
"I'm Troubled," The Watson Family
"On Top of Old Smokey," The Morris
   Brothers, North Carolina (Rounder)

The Great Migration, 1900-1945

New Departures

"Blue Railroad Train," The Delmore
   Brothers, Alabama (County)
"Brakeman's Blues," Jimmie Rodgers,
   Mississippi (RCA)
"California Blues," Jimmie Rodgers
"Gambling Polka Dot Blues," Jimmie
   Rodgers
"Blue Yodel #9," Jimmie Rodgers
"Night in a Blind Tiger," The Skillet Lickers,
   Georgia (County)

Hard Times

"My Clinch Mountain Home," The Carter
   Family, Virginia (RCA)
"Waiting for a Train," Jimmie Rodgers
"All In Down & Out Blues," Dave Macon,
   Tennessee (RBF)
"I Ain't Got No Home in This World
   Anymore," Woody Guthrie, Oklahoma
   (RCA)
"Wabash Cannonball," Roy Acuff,
   Tennessee (Columbia)
"Hobo Bill's Last Ride," Jimmie Rodgers
"Great Speckled Bird," Roy Acuff
"Wreck on the Highway," Roy Acuff

Oh say, did you see him, it was ear-ly this morning? He
passed by your houses on his way to the coal. He was tall, he was
slender and his dark eyes so tender, his occu-pation was mining, West Virginia his home.

The West Virginia Mine Disaster

This song reflects Jean Ritchie's childhood experience of conditions in the coal mining areas of Appalachia. Written commercially for a larger public audience later in her life, it illuminates a way of life still common in many parts of West Virginia, Ohio, and Kentucky. As a historical record, it also reveals the meaning of that way of life to someone who wishes to preserve its memory for subsequent generations. What do the lyrics of the song suggest, for example, about relations among different families in the mining community, or about the nature of the individual family, or about possibilities and expectations of social mobility?

2.
It was just before noon, I was feeding the children,
Ben Mosely came running to give us the news:
Number Eight was all flooded, many men were in danger
And we don't know their number, but we fear they're all doomed.

3.
I picked up the baby and I left all the others,
To comfort each other and to pray for their own;
There is Tommy, fourteen, and John not much younger,
Their time is soon coming to go down the dark hole.

4.
Oh what will I say to his poor little children,
O what will I tell his old mother at home?
And what will I say to this heart that's clear broken,
To this heart that's clear broken if my darling is gone?

5.
If I had the money to do more than just feed them,
I'd give them good learning, the best to be found,
So when they growed up they'd be checkers and weighers,
And not spend their whole lives in the dark underground.

Community History

introduction

Community history breaks down many barriers. It asks students to take a long hard look at themselves and their relation to the institutions, values, and traditions of the surrounding area. It draws on unfamiliar sources in familiar environments, requiring skills and insights from a variety of disciplines. It involves all levels of the educational process. It translates antiquarian and genealogical detail into immediate realities of life, birth, death, marriage, work, and play.

Community history may include investigation of localities beyond the direct experience of students or teachers. By examining such fundamental units of social life as wards, neighborhoods, villages, towns, and cities in different eras and parts of the world, teachers can help students to appreciate better not only their own cultural roots but also the broader forces at work in human society. Exploration of a town or city presents a case study to test the validity and variety of large and often nebulous textbook generalizations about such subjects as social control, religious influence, and political participation. As case studies accumulate, patterns emerge from actual developments rather than pre-conceived theory; connections become apparent that offer the comparative perspectives so frequently lacking in traditional history.

Community history makes more demands on teachers and students than the study of larger political entities. Close analysis of a community shows how unsatisfactory it usually is to organize history around a few famous dates, battles, and turning points. It is necessary to develop new criteria for categorizing information and look beyond conventional documentary research to the methods of archaeology, anthropology, demography, and sociology. Most of all, community history gets teachers and students out of the classroom and school into alliances with local institutions and groups that themselves can add significantly to the educational process.

Pieter Bruegel, "The Wedding Dance in the Open Air"

RELEVANCE IN YOUR OWN BACKYARD

Hazel L. Varella supervises an extensive local history program for the social studies department at Oliver Ames High School in Easton, Massachusetts. The core of the program is a course, originally organized by Duncan B. Oliver, which is elected by half the senior class each year.

In all fields of endeavor there are spectators and participants. Although "spectating" may be more popular, participating offers special rewards. History is no exception. Local History students at Oliver Ames High School do a lot of looking, but they also do more. They are personally and intimately involved in putting together a composite picture of Easton's history. The work done by each year's class broadens the base of data from which the next year's class can work. More than 1800 slides, largely prepared by students, have been assembled for use in the course. These include pictures in private collections as well as those owned by the local historical society. Students use these old images as references, photographing the same locations today and thus recording the changes time has wrought. Many documents, town records, and news clippings have been reprinted or preserved on microfilm for use by our Local History class and others. Five complete sets of town reports have been gathered as a result of our school's appeal for donations.

On the surface, group activities in Local History do not appear to be particularly different from those characteristic of any other good social studies class: reading, examining slides and photographs, listening to lectures, and discussion. A closer glance, however, reveals some significant differences. First, the students deal as much as possible with primary sources of information. Inquiry, forming and testing hypotheses, acting as one's own historian — these are integral features of the course. Second, students frequently go out into the community in organized field trips and on individual exploration. Such extensive on-site observation and investigation would not be possible in the study of any other kind of history.

Each student is required to complete an individual project during the second half of the semester, requiring at least fourteen hours of work outside the classroom. Students are encouraged to find a medium in which they feel comfortable and can use their skills. The girl who becomes intrigued with the local cemetery may make rubbings of headstones, but she will probably also identify the type of stone, its age and quarry source, and the meanings of the symbols and epitaphs carved on it; the data she gathers may help another student to fill in a gap in a genealogical record he is piecing together. Another student may trace the route of a dried-up canal bed and put together a map showing the old commercial and industrial sites served by the canal. Still another may comb an area with a metal detector, hoping to uncover long-buried iron artifacts. One way of digging up the past is to look for buried items; another is to inter-

Local History Checklist

I. To Begin

A. Contact your local historical society. If none exists, try to encourage the organization of one.

B. Collect town reports. Request copies through local newspapers. (Also check to see how extensive the back files are at the local newspaper.)

C. Copies of early town records are available up to 1840 from the Church of Jesus Christ of Latter Day Saints (contact Genealogical Society in Weston.) Remember to use cemeteries for data.

D. Use your local registry of deeds (county). See page 36.

E. Develop a community resources file.

F. Check with your community and school libraries regarding materials they have.

G. Investigate media possibilities: cameras, videotapes, recorders, etc.

H. Work with or encourage the establishment of an historic commission.

II. To Improve

A. When you have the opportunity, spend some time in the State Archives. Available items include early town maps, census data, documents relating to your community, etc.

B. Visit the New England Genealogical Society in Boston. It has data indexed by towns.

C. Begin microfilming pertinent material. A microfilm camera retails for about $1500, and is a good investment.

D. Organize a picture or slide file.

E. Determine a means of communicating with the community: e.g., newspaper column. Make requests there for materials to borrow. BE SURE TO **ACKNOWLEDGE** and **RETURN** all items.

F. Encourage independent study projects. Try to find a means of disseminating the reports.

G. Encourage student involvement with the community: interviewing town officials, the elderly, etc. Recording some of these interviews would underline the importance of PRESERVING THE PRESENT.

view elderly residents, recording their recollections and impressions, or perhaps to research the prior ownership of their land at the local Registry of Deeds.

It is very important that the information students gather be shared with the community, through newspaper columns, newsletters, and other means. In this way, Local History has done much to perpetuate good community-school relations. The activities of Local History students have caught the attention of the townspeople, whose reaction has been extremely favorable. Older residents, town officials, and businesspeople have made available their homes, facilities, personal records, and memorabilia to inquiring students. Furthermore, the program has stimulated a revival of the local historical society, which has grown to over 500 members of all ages.

Above and below, scenes from turn-of-the-century Easton, in the collection of the Easton Historical Society

There can be no question that Local History students develop a deeper understanding of history than their peers in courses relying mainly on pre-digested secondary sources with pre-determined answers to pre-arranged questions. Our students also achieve a sense of personal accomplishment in having done something unique and related to their own special interests.

D.B.O.

H.L.V.

RESOURCES FOR LOCAL HISTORY

The program at Oliver Ames High School described on the previous two pages offers a model for involving students in the history of their own community. Below, Robert Dalzell of Williams College shows one way that New England teachers interested in local history can venture further afield and draw on the resources of a community preservation project.

I have tried to take advantage of the unusual facilities offered by Historic Deerfield to develop a college program that investigates the development of a New England town as a cluster of institutions over a period of more than 250 years. This is possible at Williams — and at some other schools — because we have a four-one-four term system that permits us to move students off campus during all or part of January.

We spend the first week in Williamstown reading up on background information, and then all go to Deerfield for a two-week stay. On successive days during the first week there, I introduce the students to different kinds of evidence. One day we will deal with town records, on other days with family papers, architecture, furniture, and the like. At each morning session, along with members of the Historic Deerfield education staff. I discuss how to use these materials as evidence. Then in the afternoon there is a short research project for each student to work on individually. At a final meeting at the end of the day students report on the results of their research.

During the second week, having become familiar with the available evidence, the students examine the history of Deerfield by concentrating on a series of dates over the past centuries. Again using an in-

dividualized research format, we try to reconstruct as nearly as we can some sense of what was happening in the town during the years chosen. One student will investigate a building of a particular period, another will study the furniture, another will be assigned family materials. As before, we schedule sessions late each day where

students can report to each other.

What happens, as a result, is first that the students develop an acute understanding of what it meant to live somewhere like Deerfield — the scale of life, how it felt to reside in a place where there was just one street, a mile long, and everyone could walk everywhere, all the while being very much out in the elements. They come to see how it must have felt to spend time in rooms of the dimensions of early eighteenth-century houses, and to decide what features of that particular way of living they like and dislike.

Next, I think they learn how to approach the problem of reconstructing the past, using a variety of different kinds of evidence as imaginatively as possible to answer a wide range of questions.

Finally, the students grow to appreciate that a place like Deerfield — which seems frozen in time — really has had a continuous life. It has changed over time,

---

The County Registry of Deeds

The County Registry of Deeds can provide valuable primary source material about one's town. Deeds often include information concerning families, occupations, land, and buildings. The older the deed, the more it is apt to include.

Registries are equipped with two sets of indexes: a GRANTEE index, listing alphabetically the purchasers of property, and a GRANTOR index, listing sellers. These indexes are usually alphabetized and bound in volumes by periods of several years.

To start research, one needs to know someone who owned a piece of land and the approximate year of purchase. The person's name is looked up in the grantee index that covers that year. The index should show from whom the land was purchased (the grantor), the date of purchase, the general location of

the land, and the book and page number of the actual deed. Then one looks up the grantor (seller) in the grantee index to find from whom he or she bought the land.

Theoretically, this is all that is necessary to trace land back to the Indians. If the grantee index should fail you, it may help to look up the last actual deed of which you are aware. Other possibilities, if problems arise, are to consult the grantor index for relevant information, or to turn to probate records at probate court to see if the land was willed or involved in other legal action. County and town maps in the 1800's frequently included houses and names of owners; copies are often available at registries. Look up the house you are checking and then check the name in the grantee index. With the assistance of maps, deeds, and friendly registry personnel, you should be able to get back well over 150 years.

Hazel L. Varella

even if the larger forces shaping its development have made only a slight physical impression. It was a prosperous agricultural

Aaron G. Fryer

community in the eighteenth century; subsequently, as farming became less profitable, the town fell on hard times. Then, beginning about 100 years ago, people arrived who were in fact refugees from congested urban centers. One can see how these people participated in the life of the place, and how they worked out a balanced pattern of interaction acceptable to the farmers whose town it had been. Thus, Deerfield was touched in many significant ways by broader historical movements with which we are all familiar.

From my point of view, this program has proved very satisfactory. The only problem that I should report arises when I go back to Williamstown to teach in the regular spring term. A feeling of despair invariably comes over me when I walk into my first class. How on earth do I simply sit here in this room for 75 minutes each day to teach a

course? Surely nothing can happen in this setting, because so much has happened elsewhere.

R.D.

George French

Local History Clearinghouse

For primary, middle, and high schools in Massachusetts and other New England states, teaching and learning local history is not an option; it is REQUIRED by state law. In an effort to help teachers stay abreast of this growing field, a clearing-house has been established for projects and materials on local history, sponsored by the Bay State Historical League, Bentley College, and other institutions. For information, contact Paul Tedesco, 219 Cushing Hall, Northeastern University, Boston, Massachusetts 02115, or Patricia O'Malley at the BSHL, G.A.R. Memorial Room 27, State House, Boston, Massachusetts 02133.

Materials for Local Historians

—published local histories
—military records
—family histories
—street directories
—telephone books
—maps, atlases, gazetteers
—travellers' accounts
—business records
—sermons and anniversary talks
—photographs
—tape interviews
—private diaries, letters, account books
—keepsakes, heirlooms, relics
—newspapers
—census reports
—deeds, probate inventories, court records
—town, school, church records
—cemetery inscriptions

Guides to Local History

For specific nuts-and-bolts of local history projects, the Resource Learning Laboratory at Old Sturbridge Village (under the direction of Alberta P. Seabolt) has published a 40-page mimeographed guide, **Localized History through the Use of Community Resources**. It is especially helpful in showing how to coordinate topics, problems, resource materials, and learning techniques. For details on community history at Old Sturbridge Village, see **Social Education** (November-December, 1975).

Another introduction to the why's and wherefore's of community history is Clifford Lord's **Teaching History with Community Resources** (1964). In general terms this guide gives a rationale for local history, explaining its limitations and possibilities, and comments on specific topics, resources, projects, site visits, films, tapes, surveys, and programs.

MAINE FOLK CULTURE

High school students in Kennebunk, Maine, study history by observing and recording it. They speak with loggers, fishermen, farmers, and other local residents to investigate their state's folk culture. They transmit what they learn about lobstering, sea moss pudding, stone walls, rum running, maple syrup, snowshoes and other Yankee doings through a magazine they produce called Salt. *Many of the articles have recently been collected in* The Salt Book (1977), *edited by their advisor, Pamela Wood. To aid teachers wishing to organize similar projects in their own communities, Wood has also written* You and Aunt Arie: A Guide to Cultural Journalism Based on Foxfire and Its Descendents (1975). *Below, Wood describes* Salt — *the project, the magazine, and the book.*

In 1972 the first of the famous *Foxfire* books was published, a remarkable volume compiled from the writings of high-school students who documented the lives of their southern Appalachian relatives. In the introduction to that book, Eliot Wigginton, who shepherded the *Foxfire* books into existence, made an eloquent plea for reforging the links between students and their culture:

"Daily our grandparents are moving out of our lives, taking with them, irreparably, the kind of information contained in this book . . . . When they're gone, the magnificent hunting tales, the ghost stories that kept a thousand children sleepless, the intricate tricks of self-sufficiency acquired through years of trial and error, the eloquent and haunting stories of suffering and sharing and building and healing and planting and harvesting — all these go with them, and what a loss.

Jay York

Anne Pierter

"If this information is to be saved at all, for whatever reason, it must be saved now; and the logical researchers are the grandchildren . . . . In the process, these grandchildren [and we] gain an invaluable, unique knowledge about their own roots, heritage, and culture."

Since that time scores of student projects similar in spirit to *Foxfire* have sprung up across the country. *Salt* was the first New England attempt, beginning its fledgling life in the summer of 1973. Just as *Foxfire* succored a dozen successors, so have these successors nurtured new periodicals and books until today the number grows almost weekly.

And each of them comes in response to our compelling need for the human answers

a technological society cannot give us. In this sense, *The Foxfire Book, The Salt Book*, and the host of younger periodicals are eminently modern, eminently timely. People who put the stamp of nostalgia upon

---

"Three of us went up to see one man, early in the morning. We thought it was great, because we could get out of school if we were going to do this. He said that he couldn't talk with us, that he had to go out and pick vegetables, but if you get the rest of the day off and help me pick vegetables, I'll be glad to talk. We picked vegetables all day and interviewed him, and that is where we got the basic elements for a story. Now we go back to him, and take new people to see him."

— **Salt** student

---

them mistake their underlying intent. The real subject matter of these publications is how people cope with living, and that subject matter will forever be current. At their core is the belief that students grow stronger as they reforge their links with the culture and the people of their own community.

The essence of our magazine *Salt* consists of documented interviews with distinctive older people whose roots run deeper and whose memories reach back farther than those of everybody else. *Salt* seeks to reflect the cultural variety and richness of present-day communities in Maine, from seacoast villages to logging towns to blueberry regions to potato lands, from "old salts" to French Canadian settlers to descendants of native Indian tribes.

Using *Salt* as a training project, students learn valuable skills that prepare them for future jobs and increase their competence as functioning adults, no matter what

their job choices may be. Among those skills are writing, interviewing, transcribing, photography, darkroom techniques, page layout and design, archival management, and business methods.

Because the magazine is student-run, it offers young people chances to develop the kind of judgment they must exercise if they are to become strong adults. Students weigh options and make choices, learning by their mistakes.

The search for human values is a significant part of the experience *Salt* gives students. In the course of their interviews with older people in the community, new values are rediscovered, traditional values reexamined. Pride in roots grows. The rich alliance between young and old is reborn as youth looks to age for knowledge and wisdom and humor.

P.W.

Adapted from **Salt** (June, 1976) and **The Salt Book** by Pamela Wood (copyright © SALT 1974, 1975; copyright © SALT, Inc., 1975, 1976, 1977; reprinted by permission Doubleday and Co., Inc.)

"I got a story from a man who about thirty years ago used to go tuna fishing on a sailboat. Everything is power now, and he said there was a lot more action when he was going on a sailing vessel. I'd been around water all my life, and still found out something. I think if I kept on doing this magazine until I was 45, I would still be learning."

— **Salt** student

TOWN AND GOWN

School projects exploring local history can benefit from creative alliances with other individuals, groups, and institutions in the community. One approach is to coordinate efforts by high school and college teachers. Here is one model for such coordination; based on the Yale-New Haven History Educa- *tion Project, it is applicable to the teaching of many subjects besides the history of the particular community in which it might be implemented. A different approach, also described on this page, involves students in historical preservation and surveys.*

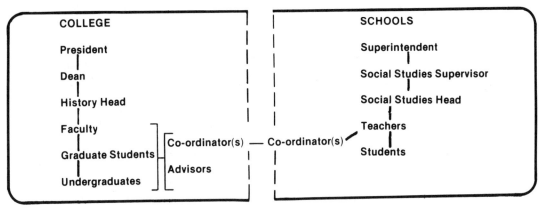

Through the Co-ordinators and Advisors, the College is responsible for:
    seeking funds to supplement school budgets
    arranging library use by school teachers
    giving academic credit for teacher certification, if necessary
    giving school teachers access to all college functions, courses, lectures
    compiling short, graded bibliographies of materials for school teachers
    visiting schools weekly.
    setting up summer workshops and summer pay for school teachers
    publishing curriculum guides
    supplying large interpretive problems and themes for possible classroom use

Under the guidance of the Supervisor and Department Head, the high school teachers are responsible for:
    reviewing, revising, and developing new history courses or teaching units
    exchanging ideas on classroom teaching methods
    selecting proper materials for student use
    attending summer workshops and periodic review sessions
    arranging teaching schedules and AV equipment
    supplying the content for curriculum guides
    filing outlines of new course units with other schools

SURVEYING AND PRESERVING THE PAST

High school and college students can often contribute significantly to the study and preservation of historic sites and districts, even though many such projects traditionally are handled in schools of design and urban planning. Teachers interested in having students identify sites for the National Register of Historic Places should contact their state historical commission. The Massachusetts State Historical Commission (State House, Boston, Massachusetts 02133) provides a series of helpful guides giving instructions and standardized forms for inventorying buildings, monuments, archaeological sites, and burying grounds. An example of a completed building survey form is on the page opposite. Surveys of individual sites and structures can form the basis of more ambitious school projects aimed at studying and preserving entire historic districts. Often these can be organized in cooperation with local historical commissions, local historical societies, regional planning agencies, or urban renewal authorities. Teachers and students interested in such large-scale surveys might consult the Cambridge Historical Commission's excellent five volume *Survey of Architectural History in Cambridge* (1965-1977). Each volume covers one of the city's five distinctive neighborhoods and includes discussion of survey procedures and forms, an essay on the historical development of the area, a typology of architectural styles, and detailed street-by-street commentary (with photographs) of residential, public, and industrial buildings.

FORM B - STRUCTURE SURVEY
MASSACHUSETTS HISTORICAL COMMISSION
Office of the Secretary, State House, Boston

2. Town _BOSTON_

Street _COPLEY SQUARE_

Name _TRINITY CHURCH_

Original Use _CHURCH_

Present Use _CHURCH_

Present Owner _WARDENS AND VESTRY_

1. Is this structure historically significant to:
   Town (Commonwealth) (Nation)

   Structure has historical connection with the
   following themes: (See also reverse side)

Agriculture	Commerce/Industry
(Architecture)	Science/Invention
(Art/Sculpture)	Travel/Communication
Education	Military Affairs
Government	(Religion)/Philosophy
Literature	Indians
Music	Development of Town/City

Date _1877 & 1897_ Style _ROMANESQUE_
CHURCH..." (see revrse)
Source of Date _ROMIG, "THE STORY OF TRINITY_

Architect _H. H. RICHARDSON_

3. CONDITION: (Excellent) Good Fair Deteriorated Moved (Altered) _WEST PORCH ADDED 1897_

   IMPORTANCE of site to area: (Great) Little None   SITE endangered by _____

4. DESCRIPTION

FOUNDATION/BASEMENT: High (Regular) Low   Material: _GRANITE_
DEDHAM GRANITE

WALL COVER: Wood _____   Brick (Stone) Other _LONGMEADOW FREESTONE_

STORIES: 1 (2) 3 4   CHIMNEYS: 1 2 3 4   Center End Cluster Elaborate Irregular

ATTACHMENTS: (Ell) Shed Wings (Dependency) _____ Simple (Complex)

ROOF: (Ridge) Gambrel Flat Hip Mansard _INTERSECTING_
_3_ (Tower) Cupola Dormer windows Balustrade (Grillwork) _LARGE CENTRAL TOWER; 2 WEST_
ENTRY

FACADE: Gable End: (Front) (Side) (Symmetrical) Asymmetrical Simple (Complex) (Ornament)

Entrance: (Front) Side (Centered) Double Features: _TRIPLE ENTRANCE WEST PORCH; ELABORATE_
SCULPTURE

Windows: Spacing: (Regular) /Irregular Identical (Varied) _STAINED GLASS - SEE REVERSE_
EXTENSIVE USE OF ENGLISH & FRENCH

Corners: (Plain) Pilasters Quoins (Obscured) _ON WEST FRONT BY PORCH_

OUTBUILDINGS _PARISH HALL + CLOISTERS-DEPENDENCY_ LANDSCAPING _GARTH ADDED IN CLOISTERS_

MEDIA PRODUCTIONS ON MAINE HISTORY

Maine forms the laboratory for an Individualized History Media Course taught by C. Stewart Doty of the University of Maine at Orono. Students have investigated the Penobscot Expedition of 1779, colonial Pemaquid, the construction of Maine's railroads, the Shakers of Sabbathday Lake, Maine lumbermen between 1900 and 1920, Acadians in the St. John Valley, and other local history topics.

Each student creates a slide-tape or videotape based on research in primary sources. Doty encourages the students to select subjects that do not lend themselves to traditional narrative treatment, but which instead require visualization. The projects are short, simple, and inexpensive, requiring equipment owned by most colleges and high schools. Each student creates a ten-minute show. Slide-tapes consist of 50-75 slides and a script on 3x5 cards that can be read along with the visual images or transfered to audiotape and sychronized.

The completed productions are preserved as instructional tools for use in other classes at the University of Maine. In this way, they become resources for others studying the state's history. A number of the productions which have been converted into sound filmstrips can be purchased through the History Media Center, University of Maine, Orono, Maine 04473.

Here are two of Doty's basic techniques for producing slide-tapes:

Here is an excerpt from a slide-tape on Maine in the Civil War edited and produced by Cynthia MacDonald:

1. The Maine volunteer was capitvataed by the idea of war, but he knew nothing about it except that there was one going on. And it had better be won!!!

Scripting: The initial script is done on 3x5 cards, divided in half by a line to form two 1½ x 1½ blocks. On the left hand side of the card the student-creator describes or sketches the visual. If the production uses two images, the left side of the card is again split by a line. On the right hand side of the card, the student writes down the music, narration, or narration over music that will accompany that particular visual. By putting the script first on cards, the creator can re-arrange the visuals, substitute one visual for another, change the sound track to better fit a particular visual, and time the production before final scripting. The final arrangement of the 3x5 cards is then transferred to scripting sheets.

Audiotaping: This is the most difficult step technically, and most students will require considerable instruction and pratice. If you do not have a campus radio station or television studio where you can mix music and voice directly onto the monophonic cassette tape, you can use a reel-to-reel stereophonic tape recorder. By taping the music on one channel and the voice on the other, you can create "voice-over-music" (i.e., music as background to the spoken word) by using the balance control to mix the two as you play back and re-record the tape onto the monophonic cassette. The biggest problem for students to overcome in taping is making sure that the voice is sufficiently louder than the music to be understood. This problem can be solved with some practice exercises in mixing during the general instruction on this step.

C.S.D.

For more information about Doty's course and his techniques, see his article "Organizing an Individualized History Media Production Course," in *Social Studies* (July-August, 1976).

2. When the excitement of the war died down, some new *incentive* was needed to raise the required number of men; and there was nothing like money to do this! This payment of money to get men to enlist was called "bounties."

3. "A dollar was hard to come by in Maine and if a man could be patriotic and lay a little away at the same time, he might as well. The smart thing to do was shop around for the highest bid; then enlist!"

4. If a man did not wish to go in the draft, he could pay a substitute to take his place. Or there was another way.

5. "Up here in Aroostook, among us old folk the common meanin' of "skedaddler" is a deserter who slipped over the line into Canada."

THE URBAN LANDSCAPE

The previous pages have concentrated on the history of some of New England's smaller communities. But New England is also heavily urbanized, and its cities may serve as learning laboratories for history classes. Below, Elizabeth S. Blackmar of the Joint Center for Urban Studies of M.I.T. and Harvard explores the social dynamics of the urban landscape.

Cities are the most complex and least understood of man-made environments. In studying them, urban historians have in the last decade begun to look beyond the accomplishments of individuals and elite groups to the experiences of whole populations. Yet for all the heightened interest in the larger social arena of the past, these historians have failed effectively to translate demographic and economic trends into a spatial dimension. On the other hand, historical geographers studying cities appreciate the importance of space; but in concentrating on analysis of generalized land use and residential patterns, they have neglected questions of power and policy — who controlled and who shaped the environment? Who received the profits from early speculative building; what assumptions, aspirations, and materials influenced design solutions; at what point did an owner of inner city property cease to feel personal responsibility for its condition and use and begin to regard it more as an investment or commodity than as a possession or an emblem or identity? When did middlemen and agents assume their roles as the brokers of public space?

Further to understand the relation of class to the urban environment requires looking beyond issues of control and ownership. City residents have made inherited space distinctly their own, giving neighborhoods cultural and organizational characteristics that supercede the concept of ownership as a means of defining status in relation to the landscape. Sam Bass Warner in *Streetcar Suburbs: The Process of Growth in Boston, 1870-1900* (1962) offers a useful model for history teachers seeking to integrate the physical development of the city with social and economic change, and to address larger questions of class and control.

A related approach to understanding the urban landscape is to examine the history of specific features of the city — its buildings, streets, open spaces, and parks. These physical forms offer an index to collective social purposes. For example, students looking at changes in street or highway design, paving, or regulation can discover the role of innovation and experimentation in forming the urban landscape. At the same time, they may encounter the limits of society's flexibility and willingness to adapt to new conditions. It is important to remember that even the most prosaic urban features — from sewers to utilities — involve the relation of different groups to the city. Throughout the nineteenth century, such basic urban amenities as internal plumbing, electric lighting, or paving and curbing were distributed according to the ability of their consumers to pay. These commonplace features can also acquire meaning beyond their practical functions, as seen in the multiple uses of streets throughout history for marketing, play, public tributes, and confrontations.

Perhaps the most obvious features of the urban landscape are its buildings and structures. Several models exist for architectural history that go beyond identifying sources of design elements or particular schools of architectural style. Charles Lockwood in *Bricks and Brownstones: New York Row Houses, 1783-1929* (1972) balances an appreciation of design against a recognition of the social forces behind its repeated modifications. Similarly, Alan Trachtenberg's *Brooklyn Bridge: Fact and Symbol* (1965) sets that dramatic structure in both the practical and the symbolic context of dynamically expanding New York City. Carl Condit's two-volume *American Building Art* (1960-1961) suggests how urban history can be understood through examination of the building industry itself.

Yet it is impossible to appreciate the evolution of urban space merely by sitting in a library reading about the past. To understand the urban landscape we must participate in it. Student and teachers must learn to observe the space around them, to see what is there and inquire where it came from. By walking the city, we can start to think about the spatial impact of such social forces as population growth and mobility, or the particular problems of traffic, or the cultural expression of different urban groups through their use of space. Where historical forms of the city have been permanently lost, we must turn to the visual and descriptive record of archives — maps, drawings, photographs, personal accounts, and documents. Once we have observed the landscape closely, we can ask deeper questions about the process of its formation.

E.S.B.

Adapted from **Journal of Architectural Education** (September, 1976).

THE CITY AS CLASSROOM

The City of Lowell, Massachusetts, has recently become the focus of intensive historical scholarship and teaching. Mary Blewett, of the University of Lowell, reports below on a conference held in Lowell in the fall of 1976 to explore the historical resources of the community.

Co-sponsored by the University of Lowell and the Lowell Historical Society, "Historic Lowell: The City as Classroom" was designed to encourage use of Lowell history in middle school, secondary school, and college curricula. The conference celebrated the 150th anniversary of the incorporation of the city, which was also marked by the opening of the new Lowell Museum and publication by the historical society of a new history of the city, *Cotton Was King* (1976).

There were several conference workshops. "The Lowell Area as an Educational Resource" considered how the Lowell Museum, the Dracut State Forest, and the physical environment of the city might be of benefit to the educational community. "The Student and the City" focused on how students relate to the past and present of Lowell, and what middle class suburban as well as inner-city working class students can learn from the urban experience.

Participants in "Lowell as a Curriculum and Focus of Research" discussed courses developed at universities using Lowell as a base and what graduate research is in progress. Possible adaptations of these ideas to other educational levels were also explored. One workshop aimed at "Retrieving the Ethnic Experience with Music and Film," while another presented advice by archivists and authors on how to find and publish local materials.

"Architecture and the Urban Life of Lowell" showed how homes, buildings, and physical space in Victorian Lowell reflected patterns of urban life and activity characteristic of that period.

Finally, participants in "The City of Lowell as a Park" discussed ways to draw on the grounds and resources of the State Heritage Park and the Urban National Park in their teaching. All sessions were tape-recorded, and are available for public use at the North Campus Library, University of Lowell.

Among teachers who have developed courses around the resources of the city, besides myself, are Charles Hill of Lowell High School, Gary Murphy of Greater Lowell Vocational Technical High School, Tom Malone of Pawtucket Memorial School, Jill Parker of Rogers School, and Brian Mitchell of Continuing Education at the University of Lowell.

M.B.

— — — — — — — — — — — —

In teaching his course on community history at the University of Lowell, Brian Mitchell combines reading assignments with tours, slide presentations, and visits by outside speakers — including members of different ethnic groups in Lowell, the city's long-range planner, and directors of the Lowell Museum. Mitchell divides the history of the city into four periods and covers the following topics:

I. PRE-INDUSTRIAL LOWELL

   A. New England and the Merrimack Valley, 1600-1800

   B. The Settlement at Chelmsford; the Middlesex Canal

II. WHEN COTTON WAS KING

   A. Origins and Early Development of the Textile Industry: The Founding of Lowell — the Plan and its implementation

   B. Textile Technology

   C. The Labor System

   D. Lowell: The Pattern of Growth

   E. Decline and the Post-Civil War Era

   F. Lowell as a Mill Town — A Unique Experiment or the First of Its Type?

III. THE IMMIGRANT EXPERIENCE

   A. The Coming of the Irish: End of an Idyll

   B. Other Post-Civil War Arrivals, I

   C. Other Post-Civil War Arrivals, II

   D. Lowell as an Immigrant City

IV. TWENTIETH-CENTURY LOWELL

   A. The End of the Mill Era

   B. Prospects for Future Development

B.M.

THE BOSTON EXPERIENCE

Over the past two summers Allen Wakstein and colleagues from Boston College, along with guest lecturers, have been offering an institute called "The Boston Experience." Through lectures, readings, guided tours, workshops, and special projects, the course examines Boston's growth from a small town on a confining peninsula to an urban center for a diverse hinterland to a modern metropolitan region. Students and teachers in the program try to increase their appreciation of a complex and beautiful city and to discover what is distinctive about its character and problems.

In particular, what is the social and cultural impact when people move from one neighborhood to another? What problems do families experience as they leave immigrant ghettoes for outlying "zones of emergence" and in subsequent generations move to suburban communities? How does residential mobility affect the family roles of women and their position in the job market? How do children react in moving from homogeous neighborhoods to those with greater heterogeneity? How do older people feel at being left behind when their children move to suburbia? How do suburban communities react to the new arrivals?

The following outline and examples of field trips show the concerns of the Institute in greater detail. In addition, Wakstein and his associates have formulated plans to offer similar programs in the Boston and suburban school systems, for teacher training or in a variety of special formats for interested groups.

INTRODUCTION

In Search of a City and Its Meaning

PART I FROM PURITAN TO PATRIOT

The Puritan Tradition

The Yankee Trader

The Physical Setting

The Coming of the Revolution

Boston and the Revolutionary Experience
WORKSHOP:

"Boston and the Hinterland:
The Case of Concord"

The Way People Lived in Eigtheenth-Century Boston

PART II THE EVOLUTION FROM
TOWN TO CITY

Bulfinch's Boston

The Brahmin Aristocracy

The Change from Town to City
WORKSHOP:

"Prospects and Sources in
Community History"

Trade to the Seven Seas

Spindles and Looms

The Great Mayor

The Way People Lived in Jacksonian Boston

The Responsible Community

The Athens of America

The Ferment of Reform

PART III THE NEW CHALLENGES

The Coming of the New Bostonians
WORKSHOP:

"Popular Authors and Their Audiences
in Nineteenth-Century Boston"

Conflict Between Old and New

The Way People Lived in Late Nineteenth-
Century Boston

The Boom Town and Urban Imperialism

The Back Bay and Its Architecture

PART IV THE CITY IN TRANSITION

The Rise of the Ward Boss

The New Immigrants

The Genteel Tradition

The Fenway

The Efforts of the Reformers

Political Reform and the New Power

The Politics of James Michael Curley

Social and Cultural Challenges for the
Twentieth Century
WORKSHOP:

"The Media and the City"

PART V THE PROBLEMS AND PROSPECTS
OF MODERN BOSTON

The Crisis of Boston and New England

The Way People Live in Twentieth-Century
Boston

Transportation and Suburbanization

A Planner's Perspective of Boston
WORKSHOP:

"Development of Community Materials
and Their Use in the Classroom"

Building a New City: Urban Renewal
and the New Boston

Race and Minorities in Modern Boston

Boston's Changing Neighborhoods

The South End, Dorcester, and West
Roxbury

The Modern Metropolis

The Architecture of the City

The New Politics

Contemporary Problems in Historical
Perspective

A series of conducted tours permits participants in the Institute to "experience" the developments, diversity, and character of Boston during its major historical periods. Each tour is preceded by a class lecture that helps students reach beyond present forms and recreate in their imaginations the city of the past. The tours provide such visual juxtapositions as the Boston of the immigrants (North End) with the Boston of the Brahmins (Beacon Hill), the city of deteriorating dwellings (Roxbury) with that of the stately residences (Back Bay). One tour emphasizes the historical growth of the city's cultural institutions and elaborate park system (the Fenway and Emerald Necklace), while another looks at modern architecture against the traditional. A tour of the South End reveals the varied immigrant, ethnic, and racial groups that reside there, the diverse institutions that serve them and others, and the older ideal of residential community dwellings (Worcester Square) in contrast to newer efforts in housing (Inquilinos Boricuas en Acción-IBA).

Participants in "The Boston Experience" visit Inquilinos Boricuas en Acción-IBA, a new subsidized residential community. Established by South End residents, it largely serves the Hispanic population of the 1970's.

Boston 200

The sense of "community" that may prevail in small towns seems harder to discover in larger urban centers. Yet most cities are, in fact, agglomerations of smaller units, and the "neighborhood" or even the "block" may provide the best focus for urban local history. Boston provides a good example of a city based on a very complex, often uneasy alliance of small, almost isolated communities. Boston 200, during its brief Bicentennial existence, sponsored a series of pamphlets combining good historical information, photographs, and oral history interviews on sections like Mission Hill, Roslindale, the South End, South Boston, and the North End. Unfortunately, some of the pamphlets are already out of print, unavailable except at libraries, but others can be located through the Little City Halls.

Foxfire in the City

In 1975, adapting the model of the **Foxfire** project in Rabun Gap, Georgia, to an inner city environment, students at South Boston High School prepared a history of their community by interviewing senior citizens about family life, schooling, work, and leisure in the early twentieth century. The project formed the basis of a seven-week elective course entitled "Writing Our Own History of South Boston," in which 35 students (along with 25 elders) participated. The results are described by their teacher, Deborah Insell, in **English Journal** (September, 1975).

WHAT IS A COMMUNITY?

This is an obvious fundamental question that arises in any local history course. One among many ways of answering it is provided by Peter Gould and Rodney White in Mental Maps *(1974). Through surveys of students at the beginning of a course or field interviews for oral histories, it is possible to map a person's most and least familiar zones in any given geographical area. The techniques of survey-mapping suggested by Gould and White are useful in identifying those areas in any community that are psychologically inviting or forbidding. Psycho-social maps thus may be a good way to start studying a neighborhood's history, or to prepare for inter-viewing among older people in a community. Reproduced on this page, from* Mental Maps, *are images of the Mission Hill section of Boston.*

People's information about a particular area in one of America's cities may vary considerably, and the mental images they build up may reflect not only their surroundings but many other aspects of themselves and their lives. In the Mission Hill area of Boston, for example, Florence Ladd asked a number of Black children to draw a map of their area, and then she tape-

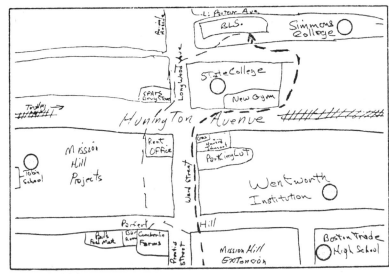

b. Ralph's map

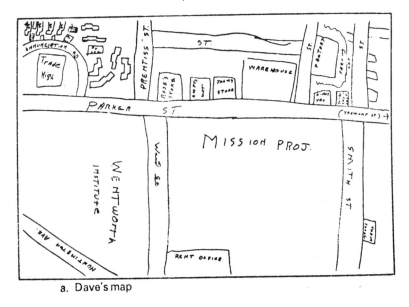

a. Dave's map

recorded her conversation with them. On Dave's map (Figure a), the Mission Hill project is where the white children live, and he has drawn it as the largest, completely blank area on his map. From his taped conversation it is clear that he is physically afraid of the area and has never ventured near it. On his map the white residential area is literally *terra incognita*, while all the detail on the map is immediately around his home and school on the other side of Parker Street. Going to the local neighborhood school, Dave has never ventured across this barrier to the unknown area beyond. However, another Black youth, Ralph, who attends the well-known Boston Latin School, draws a completely different map (Figure b). The white Mission Hill project is greatly reduced in scale, and he puts in five educational institutions in the area, indicative of his perception of education as an escape route from the segregated life he leads. Similar pieces of information are given quite different emphasis in the mental images these boys have, and the patterns of information even begin to define their neighborhoods. Dave obviously feels at home only in a quite restricted area which he knows well, while Ralph has a much wider view and allocates his information evenly across the map.

P.G.
R.W.

IF ALL THE WORLD WERE CHICAGO . . .

Whether or not one teaches in a large metropolis, it may be worthwhile to focus an urban history course on a single city at a particular time. Chicago, in the years between the two World Wars, is especially suitable. Interesting materials are available in most public and college libraries.

In the 1920's and 1930's Chicago was the center for pioneering sociological studies of urban phenomena. Probably no other city has ever been investigated in such detail. Robert Park and his colleagues at the University of Chicago used a variety of re-

search techniques, including participant observation, the collection of life histories, and quantification. Although their books have weaknesses as sociology, they become rich classroom documents when set in historical context. Among the most helpful are Nels Anderson, *The Hobo: The Sociology of the Homeless Man* (1923); Harvey Zorbaugh, *The Gold Coast and the Slum* (1929); and Clifford Shaw, *The Jack-Roller: A Delinquent Boy's Own Story* (1930). An important study of slightly later date is St. Clair Drake and Horace Cayton, *Black Metropolis: A Study of Negro Life in a Northern City* (1945).

The national media focused much attention on Chicago in the inter-war period, particularly its crime and politics. *The New Republic, Current History, Newsweek,* and other journals readily available to teachers and students ran articles with such alluring titles as "Machine guns now, what next?", "Chicago's booze war," and "Philanthropic ward boss explains an embezzlement."

Fiction is another point of entry into the history of Chicago. Willa Cather, *Lucy Gayheart* (1935), James Farrell, *Studs Lonigan: A Trilogy* (1938), and Richard Wright, *Native Son* (1940) are among the notable American novels that have been set in the Windy City. Other interesting primary sources include guide books and such government reports as the *Illinois Crime Survey* (1929) and *The Negro in Chicago* (1922).

By using maps and photographs, it is possible to study the physical development of a city without visiting it in person. For Chicago, two well-illustrated secondary works, Harold Mayer and Richard Wade, *Chicago: Growth of a Metropolis* (1969) and Carl Condit, *Chicago, 1910-1929: Building, Planning and Urban Technology*(1973),

make the task easier.

Chicago provides one good model for the study of urban history. Concentrating on a single city, one has time to zero in on particular events and people, while placing them in broader historical perspective. In the case of Chicago, it is revealing to look at the race riot of 1919, the St. Valentine's Day Massacre, the Century of Progress International Exposition of 1933-1934, Mayor "Big" Bill Thompson, Al Capone, Robert Hutchins, Carl Sandburg. The same approach can be adapted for other major American cities.

Local History in a Foreign Policy Course?

Thomas Banit at Walpole High School has integrated material from his master's thesis on Bridgeport, Connecticut, during World War I into a course on modern American foreign policy. Using city documents, census statistics on industry, employment and ethnic groupings, and newspapers, the unit relates national issues of neutrality, the draft, war, and peace to the history of a particular community where a major employer was the Remington Arms Company, owned by the Rockefellers. Economic information traces the impact of war orders and population growth. Increased employment attracted Eastern European immigrants, modifying the influence of earlier immigrants and old Yankees. Newspapers reflected shifts of public opinion, effects of propaganda, issues of loyalty, anti-war protests, and strikes. A major result was that Bridgeport workers evaded the rule of Republican bosses, bypassed the Democratic organization, and made the Socialists the major political party in the city for a generation after the war.

CITIES ACROSS THE OCEAN

Though removed in distance, culture, and perhaps time, the cities of Europe also provide opportunities for teachers in New England and their students to explore historical processes in the context of community. At the Metropolitan College Campus of Boston University, Bruce Bank teaches "The Urban Civilization of the Early Modern Period, 1300-1800," a comparative investigation of Venice, Florence, Amsterdam, Paris, and London. In tracing the evolution of cities from semi-autonomous units in late Medieval society to more or less integrated parts of national monarchical systems, Bank reaches beyond urban experience to consider other large issues in early modern European history. Among the topics he covers are the politics of the Italian City states, the relationship between cities and oceanic expansion, the interplay between monarchy and metropolis, and the nature of life in national capitals of the eighteenth century. He completes the course with a look at urban experience in the New World. Assigned readings include Fritz Rorig, *The Medieval Town* (1967); D.S. Chambers, *The Imperial Age of Venice* (1970); Gene A. Brucker, *The Society of Renaissance Florence* (1971); Orest Ranum, *Paris in the Age of Absolutism* (1968); and George Rudé, *Paris and London in the Eighteenth Century* (1970). Bank also recommends the two-volume text by F. Roy Willis, *Western Civilization: An Urban Approach* (1973).

European Reading List

The following list of readings is meant merely to be suggestive. Many of the secondary works have excellent bibliographies that can direct further exploration.

Marvin Becker, **Florence in Transition** (1968).

Andrei Biely, **St. Petersburg** (1911).

Gene Brucker, **Florentine Politics and Society, 1343-78** (1962).

Charles Booth, **Life and Labor of the People of London** (1892).

Louis Chevalier, **Laboring Classes and Dangerous Classes: In Paris During the First Half of the 19th Century** (1973).

Eric Cochrane, **Florence in the Forgotten Centuries, 1527-1800** (1973).

Geoffrey Cotterell, **Amsterdam: The Life of a City** (1972).

Pierre Couperie, **Paris Through the Ages, An Illustrated Atlas of Urbanism and Architecture** (1968).

H.J. Dyos, **The Study of Urban History** (1968).

H.J. Dyos and Michael Wolff, eds., **The Victorian City** (2 vols., 1973).

Frederic Engels, **The Condition of the Working Class in England in 1844** (1845).

T.S. Fedor, **Patterns of Urban Growth in the Russian Empire During the Nineteenth Century** (1975).

Elizabeth Gaskell, **Mary Barton** (1863).

Siegfried Giedion, **Space, Time, and Architecture** (1941).

Erwin A. Gutkind, **Urban Development in Southern Europe** (1969).

Victor Hugo, **Les Miserables** (1862).

John K. Hyde, **Padua in the Age of Dante: The Social History of an Italian City State, 1256-1328** (1966).

Jeffrey Kaplow, **The Names of Kings: The Parisian Poor in the 18th Century** (1972).

Barbara M. Lane, **Architecture and Politics in Germany, 1918-1945** (1968).

Oliver Logan, **Culture and Society in Venice, 1470-1790** (1972).

Bernd Moeller, **Imperial Cities and the Reformation** (1966).

David Pinckney, **Napoleon III and the Rebuilding of Paris** (1958).

Steen Eiler Rasmussen, **London, The Unique City** (1934).

Gareth Stedman-Jones, **Outcast London** (1972).

Mack Walker, **German Home Towns: Community, State, and General Estate, 1648-1871** (1971).

Adna Weber, **The Growth of Cities in the 19th Century** (1899).

Michael Young and Peter Willmott, **Family and Kinship in East London** (1957).

An interdisciplinary approach to European local history informs a course given at Harvard University by William Bond, J.H. Chillington, Jean Martin, and Evangeline Morphos. Under the title "All that Life Can Afford, London, 1660-1714," it covers such events as the plague, the fire, the Popish Plot, and the Glorious Revolution, drawing upon a rich array of contemporary writings by Samuel Pepys, John Locke, John Bunyan, John Dryden, Alexander Pope, Jonathan Swift, Robert Hooke, Isaac Newton, Daniel Defoe, and others. From these primary sources, students consider the urban conditions, political thought, religious ideas, scientific developments, literary satire, and art that combined to transform life at the end of England's pre-industrial period.

Artisans manufacture playing cards for seventeenth-century Parisian gamblers. The view is of the Seine, from the Louvre to Chaillot.

Personality in History

introduction

Current trends in scholarship are so various that it is difficult to be certain whether or to what extent the study of personality in history is flourishing. Although the subject of personality is of course persistent in history teaching, as an ancient concern of historians, it is vulnerable to criticism from proponents of the "new" history for its over-emphasis of individual elite actors. On the other hand, some investigators of historical personality are themselves self-styled "new" historians by virtue of their interdisciplinary excursions into Freudian and social-psychological theory, probing beneath recorded facts and rational motivations. At the same time, the humanistic psychology of Erik Erikson has prompted other scholars to reexamine the lives and minds of prominent individuals primarily in order to grapple with fundamental problems of human existence and survival. The psychohistory "movement" thus encompasses some of the most advanced methodology employed by historians and some of the most traditional humanistic concerns.

In these circumstances it is not surprising to discover that experimental history teachers in New England have been strikingly diverse in their approaches to historical personality. Especially at the college and university level, teachers are apt to focus on personality from a biographical perspective — perhaps traditional in its attention to a few outstanding figures, but sometimes methodologically esoteric as well. Most forms of psychohistorical scholarship are alive and well in history departments throughout New England (not to mention other academic disciplines, in which labor such leading scholars as Robert J. Lifton and Gerald M. Platt), and the diverse results are evident in history classrooms.

Other broadly appealing experiments in teaching historical personality should also be noted. These range from workshop or laboratory courses that try to enter an era through dramatic episodes involving relatively few individuals to the numerous exercises in historical role-playing that have had particularly important impact at the high school level. This last category of experimentation is based upon a large and complex body of role analysis and game theory in the social sciences.

Eventually, it may be predicted, the potential harmony of these various efforts to study and teach personality in history will become more apparent. Then, doubtless, this will be generally recognized as yet another area of scholarship and teaching that deserves the enviable label "new."

HISTORICAL BIOGRAPHY

The relationship between biography and history is problematic, especially in a society that purports to embody democratic principles. One New England historian from an earlier era explained the problem with a subtlety that has not been matched since.

Should history ever become a true science, it must expect to establish its laws, not from the complicated story of rival European nationalities, but from the methodical evolution of a great democracy. . . . In the fierce struggle characteristic of European society, systems were permanent in nothing except in the general law, that, whatever other character they might possess they must always be chiefly military.

The want of permanence was not the only or the most confusing obstacle to the treatment of European history as a science. The intensity of the struggle gave prominence to the individual, until the hero seemed all, society nothing; and what was worse for scientific purposes, the men interested more than the societies. In the dramatic view of history, the hero deserved more to be studied than the community to which he belonged; in truth, he was the society, which existed only to produce him and to perish with him. Against such a view historians were among the last to protest, and protested but faintly when they did so at all. They felt as strongly as their audiences that the highest achievements were alone worth remembering either in history or in art, and that a reiteration of commonplaces was commonplace. With all the advantages of European movement and color, few historians succeeded in enlivening or dignifying the lack of motive, intelligence, and morality, the helplessness characteristic of many long periods in the face of crushing problems, and the futility of human efforts to escape from difficulties religious, political, and social. In a period extending over four or five thousand years, more or less capable of historical treatment, historians were content to illustrate here and there the most dramatic moments of the most striking communities. The hero was their favorite. War was the chief field of heroic action, and even the history of England was chiefly the story of war.

The history of the United States promised to be free from such disturbances. War counted for little, the hero for less; on the people alone the eye could permanently rest. The steady growth of a vast population without the social distinctions that confused other histories, — without kings, nobles, or armies; without church, traditions, and prejudices, — seemed a subject for the man of science rather than for dramatists or poets. To scientific treatment only one great obstacle existed. Americans, like Europeans, were not disposed to make of their history a mechanical evolution. They felt that they even more than other nations needed the heroic element, because they breathed an atmosphere of peace and industry where heroism could seldom be displayed; and in unconscious protest against their own social conditions they adorned with imaginary qualities scores of supposed leaders, whose only merit was their faculty of reflecting a popular trait. Instinctively they clung to ancient history as though conscious that of all misfortunes that could befall the national character, the greatest would be the loss of the established ideals which alone ennobled human weakness. Without heroes, the national character of the United States had few charms of imagination even to Americans . . .

Whether the scientific or the heroic view were taken, in either case the starting-point was the same, and the chief object of interest was to define national character. Whether the figures of history were treated as heroes or as types, they must be taken to represent the people. American types were especially worth study if they were to represent the greatest democratic evolution the world could know. Readers might judge for themselves what share the individual possessed in creating or shaping the nation; but whether it was small or great, the nation could be understood only by studying the individual.

— Henry Adams, *History of the United States of America during the Administrations of Thomas Jefferson and James Madison (1889-1891)*

HENRY ADAMS ABOUT 1875

Harvard University Archives

REPRESENTATIVE AMERICANS

Various courses in schools around New England focus on American biography and autobiography, mostly following Henry Adams's cue in stressing the representativeness of the lives being considered. Some teachers supplement reading assignments with audio-visual materials, and have occasionally departed from traditional classroom format. At the University of Vermont, for example, Harold Schultz regularly shows slides of portraits to illustrate the changing appearance of each individual through all stages of his or her life. And at Springfield College Gene Rich asks students in "American Biographies" to role-play from the perspective of the personalities studied. Below, culled from a miscellany of syllabi, is a sampling of American personalities whose lives are well documented and appear representative, yet may be unfamiliar to many students and even some teachers.

Mason Locke Weems, **The Life of George Washington** (1809)

Henry Adams, **John Randolph** (1882)

Boynton Merrill, Jr., **Jefferson's Nephews: A Frontier Tragedy** (1977)

Black Hawk, **An Autobiography** (1833)

Lucy Larcom, **A New England Girlhood** (1889)

Fawn Brodie, **No Man Knows My History: The Life of Joseph Smith** (1945)

Frederick Douglass, **Narrative of the Life of an American Slave** (1845)

Martin Duberman, **James Russell Lowell** (1966)

Stephen Oates, **To Purge This Land With Blood: John Brown** (1970)

Ruth Randall, **Mary Lincoln** (1953)

Neil Harris, **Humbug: The Art of P.T. Barnum** (1973)

William F. Cody, **Adventures of Buffalo Bill** (1904)

John Niehard, ed., **Black Elk Speaks** (1932)

John Muir, **The Story of My Boyhood and Youth** (1913)

C. Vann Woodward, **Tom Watson: Agrarian Rebel** (1939)

Harold Livesay, **Andrew Carnegie and the Rise of Big Business** (1975)

Dorothy Richardson, **The Long Day: The Story of a New York Working Girl** (1905)

William Riordan, **Plunkitt of Tammany Hall** (1905)

Emma Goldman, **Living My Life** (2 vols., 1936)

Lincoln Steffens, **Autobiography** (1931)

Elizabeth Cady Stanton, **Eighty Years and More, 1815-1897** (1898)

John McGraw, **My Thirty Years in Baseball** (1923)

William A. White, **Puritan in Babylon: Calvin Coolidge** (1963)

Clarence Darrow, **My Life** (1932)

Len DeCaux, **Labor Radical** (1970)

William Swanberg, **Citizen Hearst** (1961)

Richard Wright, **Black Boy** (1945)

Theodore Rosengarten, **All God's Dangers: The Life of Nate Shaw** (1974)

T. Harry Williams, **Huey Long** (1969)

Joseph Lash, **Eleanor and Franklin** (1971)

Woodie Guthrie, **Bound for Glory** (1943)

Robert Caro, **The Power Broker: Robert Moses and the Fall of New York** (1974)

Frank Capra, **The Name Above the Title** (1971)

Lillian Hellman, **Scoundrel Time** (1976)

Anne Moody, **Growing Up in Mississippi** (1968)

Malcolm X, **The Autobiography of Malcolm X** (1965)

Richard Nixon, **Six Crises** (1962)

EUROPEAN LIVES

European history courses devoted specifically to the subject of personality appear to be less common than such American courses, and more diverse in their approaches. At Boston University's Metropolitan College, for example, Bruce Bank has explored a wide-ranging selection of autobiographical literature in teaching "The Emergence of the Individual in the Western World." Individuals studied have included Augustine, Héloise and Abelard, Benvenuto Cellini, Theresa of Avila, Michel de Montaigne, Jean Jacques Rousseau, Charles Darwin, and Sigmund Freud. Among the supplementary readings recommended by Bank are the following:

Margaret Bottrall, **Every Man a Phoenix: Studies in Seventeenth-Century Autobiography** (1958)

A.J. Krailsheimer, **Studies in Self-Interest from Descartes to La Bruyère** (1962)

Arnaldo Momigliano, **The Development of Greek Biography: Four Lectures** (1971)

James Olney, **Metaphors of Self: The Meaning of Autobiography** (1972)

Roy Pascal, **Design and Truth in Autobiography** (1960)

G.A. Starr, **Defoe and Spiritual Autobiography** (1965)

Owen C. Watkins, **The Puritan Experience: Studies in Spiritual Autobiography** (1972)

Less extensive in chronology but more various in its selection of topics is "The Role of Personalities in History, c. 1648-1815," an intensive pro-seminar offered at Smith College by Nelly S. Hoyt. Through both autobiographical sources and biography, Hoyt considers such subjects as seventeenth-century military leadership, "adventure" in the eighteenth century, the "personality" of crowds, and the relationship of historical personages to their legends. As a final exercise, Hoyt's students have formed into small groups for oral presentations of their research on different personalities. One such group project recreated a scene from a *salon* in Enlightenment France; another, following a script that students had developed out of primary sources, presented a conversation in a London literary club after debate in Parliament over the issue of colonial emancipation.

PERSONALITY THROUGH HISTORICAL EDITING

Ross W. Beales, Jr., has recently offered a one-semester undergraduate seminar on historical editing through the Holy Cross College Center for Experimental Studies. The purpose of the course was not to turn out historical editors but to use historical editing as a means of developing skills in research, critical analysis of primary sources, effective historical writing, interpretation, consistency, and accuracy.

The focus of the course was General Philip Schuyler, commander of the northern department of the Continental Army in the crucial summer of 1777 when Burgoyne's British forces were striking southward from Canada and before the decisive battle of Saratoga. The historical document edited by the class is a letter-book kept by Schuyler's aides that was discovered in the manuscript collections of the American Antiquarian Society in Worcester, Massachusetts. The seminar's activities required much more than creating an accurate text of the document. The students read about the general background of the Revolution; developed editorial criteria; selected, transcribed, and arranged the documents; composed general introductions, headnotes, and footnotes; visited sites along the British army's route; learned about procedures in other editing projects; and consulted collateral documents.

Intensive focus on the writings and decisions of one individual required the students to face the dilemmas of emphasis raised by studying any individual in history. How much should the scholar focus on the individual, how much on those around him or the general context of events? How to select which documents represent the individual's behavior and thinking without the bias of hindsight? How much intepretation

should editors provide?

Such questions and the larger issues they raise apply to other individuals, groups, or events that teachers and students may want to examine in similar seminars. Some of the needed information and debate about the current state of the art appears in Leslie W. Dunlap and Fred Shelley, eds., *The Publication of American Historical Manuscripts* (1973). Beales has described his project more thoroughly in "Historical Editing and Undergraduate Teaching: A Rationale and a Model," in a forthcoming issue of *Teaching History.*

Major General Philip Schuyler

Courtesy of the New-York Historical Society, New York City

PSYCHOANALYSIS AND HISTORICAL BIOGRAPHY

At Williams College, Robert G. L. Waite collaborates with a psychologist or a psychoanalyst to offer a seminar along the following lines.

The purpose of the seminar is to introduce students to problems, promises, and perils of using psychoanalysis as an aid to a fuller understanding of historical personalities.

First, students explore in common the theoretical works of two giants in the field — Freud and Erikson. The psychologist-psychoanalyst leads three or four discussions of this reading. Then two or three lecture/discussions are given by the historian to evaluate successful and unsuccessful efforts at psychobiography. Examples might include studies of Woodrow Wilson, Adolph Hitler, Leonardo da Vinci, or George III.

In the meantime, each student has chosen and begun research on a particular historical personality. This work constitutes the main concern of the seminar. A project may come from literature, politics, music, etc., as long as primary materials are available: letters, diaries, memoirs, poems, speeches. The idea is *not* to have undergraduate amateurs "psychoanalyze" their subjects or reduce the careers of important historical figures to textbook diagnosis. The more modest hope is that students will discover the *extent to which* psychology can be *helpful* in reaching a fuller understanding of historical biography. Eventually each student writes a formal essay focusing on one key problem in the life and career of his/her subject. Subjects pursued by students in recent years have included Napoleon, Kafka, Disraeli, Theodore Roosevelt, Nietzsche, Lord Byron, and Malcolm X.

R.G.L.W.

PSYCHO-QUIZ

When about sixteen years of age I happened to meet with a book written by one Tryon, recommending a vegetable diet. I determined to go into it. My brother, being yet unmarried, did not keep house but boarded himself and his apprentices in another family. My refusing to eat flesh occasioned an inconveniency, and I was frequently chid for my singularity. I made myself acquainted with Tryon's manner of preparing some of his dishes, such as boiling potatoes or rice, making hasty pudding, and a few others; and then proposed to my brother that if he would give me weekly half the money he paid for my board, I would board myself. He instantly agreed to it, and I presently found that I could save half of what he paid me. This was an additional fund for buying of books. But I had another advantage in it. My brother and the rest going from the printing house to their meals, I remained there alone, and dispatching presently my light repast (which often was no more than a biscuit or a slice of bread, a handful of raisins or a tart from the pastry cook's, and a glass of water) had the rest of the time till their return for study, in which I made the greater progress from that greater clearness of head and quicker apprehension which generally attend temperance in eating and drinking.

—The Autobiography of Benjamin Franklin

From the time that Margaret Rule first found herself to be formally besieged by the Spectres untill the Ninth Day following . . . she kept an entire Fast, and yet she was unto all appearance as Fresh, as Lively, as Hearty, at the Nine Days End, as before they began; in all this time, tho' she had a very eager Hunger upon her Stomach, yet if any refreshment were brought unto her, her Teeth would be set, and she would be thrown into many Miseries . . . . But I Pray what will you say to this, Margaret Rule would sometimes have her Jaws forcibly pulled open, whereupon something Invisible would be poured down her Throat; we all saw her swallow, and yet we saw her try all she could by Spitting, Coughing and Shriking, that she might not swallow, but one time the standers by plainly saw something of that odd Liquor it self on the outside of her Neck; She cried out of it as of Scalding Brimstone poured into her, and the whole House would immediately scent so hot of Brimstone that we were scarce able to endure it . . . .

— Cotton Mather, "The Afflictions of Margaret Rule," in George Lincoln Burr, ed., *Narratives of the Witchcraft 1648-1706* (1914).

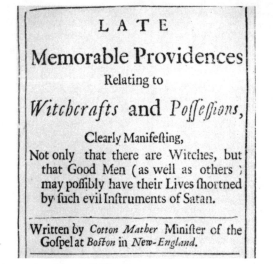

How do psychohistorians interpret evidence? The texts above illustrate the kinds of source material that teachers of psychohistory as well as researchers in this field must use. Explanations based on recent scholarship (by teachers located in New England) may be found on the following page.

PSYCHOHISTORY IN PERSPECTIVE

Philip Pomper, who teaches at Wesleyan University, comments below on the possibilities of psychohistory in the classroom. A condensed version of his own syllabus is on the facing page.

Any course on psychohistory is a new kind of course, and the problems of designing and conceptualizing such a course are not obvious. Mine is one of several offerings at Wesleyan under the rubric "Critical Approaches to History," the purpose of each in its different way being to develop theoretical sophistication in historiography and historical method.

What distinguishes psychohistory from other varieties of history? Most importantly, because of its biological basis, it is fundamentally naturalistic. Since it claims to examine the working of human nature in history, teaching us basic things about ourselves, it is also particularly prone to radical interpretation. Therefore the field of psychohistory has attracted a self-selected group of writers committed to visions that try to get at the root of things — persons, perhaps of a prophetic bent, who want to uproot evil.

Further, always at least implicit in the psychohistorical tradition is the concept of species survival — an ever-present concern of the major psychohistorical prophets even where they seem to focus on narrow historical events. In addition to species survival, psychohistory is based on concepts of sickness and health, which grow out of the medical or psychiatric tradition. Even more precisely, most practitioners of psychohistory are psychiatrists in the Freudian tradition. So not merely survival but pathology and psychological well-being enter into psychohistory, however problematically.

Among the sub-fields within psychohistory, the most familiar is psychobiography. Indeed, many people confuse the two. Psychobiography searches for the origins of a style of behavior underlying the significant contributions of historical actors. Psychobiographers are in the habit of assigning individual patterns of action to behavioral categories, such as obsessional or anal, and very often they look for a trauma that is the basis of a repetition compulsion in the behavior of a historical actor. The idea of the slow return of the repressed is crucial in many studies that reflect the more orthodox aspects of the Freudian tradition. Other psychobiographers, like Erik Erikson, are concerned more optimistically with the adaptive struggle of gifted individuals for self-realization. More generally, the psychobiographer hunts for the origins of a mode of behavior or even for a specific action that is symptomatic of a characteristic resolution of intra-psychic conflict.

Psychobiography can also be connected with community or group history. The more interesting psychobiographies do not end with the individual life history, but go on to describe the intersection of the individual's life with the history of a community or a group. The great master of this kind of psychohistory is again Erikson, who almost created the genre himself. He writes about what he calls "heroes of the inner frontier," introspective geniuses whose redemptive suffering permits the larger human group in which they act out their drama to experience a form of rejuvenation. If Erikson's introspective geniuses are heroes, the hero behind them is the human ego, whose struggle to win ground at the expense of a negative conscience or of a severe superego is central to the drama of Eriksonian psychohistory. It is a great man theory of history, as he practices it, since community crises are solved by extraordinarily gifted individuals. Before Freud, according to Erikson, psychiatry functioned through the persons of great religious figures like Luther; Ghandi, in the modern era, was similarly therapeutic.

Here it is that psychohistory intersects too, with cultural anthropology and sociology — with their questions about national or group character and the emergence of new modal personality structures in changing historical environments. The people who work in this area are frequently affiliated with the structuralist school of sociology. They believe that some kinds of social, economic, and institutional change imply other kinds of change, which eventually crystallize into a new harmony of social structure, human personality, and ideology — all associated in a single integrated system.

Yet another sub-field of psychohistory may be said to focus on psychological epidemics — that is, significant outbreaks of symptoms in a population, attributable to a traumatic event. There are also theories of more long-term cultural or social trends leading to increases in certain kinds of psychiatric disturbances, or of pathological character types that persist through several historical epochs.

Finally, the psychohistorical tradition includes metahistorical systems and their vast statements about human survival. These not only embrace traditionally defined historical periods or short-term generational problems but judge the trajectory of the human species and prescribe for the future. Of these, almost all have had to address themselves to Freud's own formulation in *Civilization and Its Discontents.*

My course begins with these metahistorical systems, and *Civilization and Its Discontents* poses the problems with its profoundly pessimistic outlook — is there an overall tendency toward an increase of guilt, toward more punitive cultural super egos? This statement of the problem and subsequent responses by psychohistorical dialecticians like Norman O. Brown and Herbert Marcuse, although accessible only through difficult and complex reading, invariably affect and engage students.

There is some advantage in raising the largest issues first and then considering the more specific problems in more specific historical contexts. At the very end of the term I return to the basic issues that I think a course in psychohistory must confront — are we on the verge of a new breakthrough, suggested by psychohistory's prophets, in the organization of human personality? This is what is on the minds of many students who take psychohistory. They are concerned, as they ought to be, with human survival. They are looking for a way out. And psychohistory is one of the areas in our curricula where prophetic readings of this sort are appropriate. They challenge students to develop theoretical sophistication, demand several kinds of mastery, and lead us the the very largest questions about the organization of human personality and its future. These questions, I think, make psychohistory, from the viewpoint of both the instructor and the student, one of the most exciting of the new approaches to history.

P.P.

Rick Stafford

Erik Erikson

Part I: Psychoanalysis and Human Salvation

1. Sigmund Freud, **Civilization and its Discontents** (1930).
   Charles Brenner, **An Elementary Textbook of Psychoanalysis** (1955).
   Sigmund Freud, **An Outline of Psychoanalysis** (1940).
2. Herbert Marcuse, **Eros and Civilization: A Philosophical Inquiry into Freud** (1955).
   Paul A. Robinson, **The Freudian Left: Wilhelm Reich, Geza Roheim, Herbert Marcuse** (1969).
3. Norman O. Brown, **Life Against Death: The Psychoanalytical Meaning of History** (1959).
4. Philip Rieff, **The Triumph of the Therapeutic** (1966).

Part II: The Problem of the Great Leader in Psychohistory

1. Sigmund Freud, **Moses and Monotheism** (1939).
   Philip Rieff, "The Meaning of History and Religion in Freud's Thought," in Bruce Mazlish, ed., **Psychoanalysis and History** (1963).
   Salo Baron, review of **Moses and Monotheism** in Mazlish, ed., **Psychoanalysis and History.**
2. Erik Erikson, **Young Man Luther** (1958).
3. Erik Erikson, **Ghandi's Truth** (1969).

Part III: Psychological Evolution and Revolution

1. Fred Weinstein and Gerald M. Platt, **The Wish to Be Free** (1969).
2. Robert J. Lifton, **Boundaries: Psychological Man in Revolution** (1969).
   _____ , "On Psychohistory," in Lifton, ed., **Explorations in Psychohistory** (1975).
3. Lloyd DeMause, "The Evolution of Childhood," in DeMause, ed., **The History of Childhood** (1974).

IS PSYCHOHISTORY TOO DIFFICULT TO TEACH?

Below, the psychohistorian Bruce Mazlish, of the Massachusetts Institute of Technology, explores the problems and possibilities of psychohistory in the classroom.

History today is faced with a paradox. At a time when it is experiencing reduced enrollments, accusations of irrelevance, and a crisis of self-confidence, it is also undergoing some of the most exciting intellectual transformations — the so-called "new approaches" — in its long history. One such new approach, of course, is psychohistory.

The paradox poses problems, for it is undeniable that a gulf is opening between the professional historian and the general public. The "new history" — whether psychological in orientation, or perhaps more commonly quantitative — imposes specialized demands on the average student that he or she cannot meet without special efforts. Thus, the interests of the scholars at the cutting edge of the profession diverge more and more sharply from the immediate concerns and capabilities of the general consumer, and will continue to do so.

Psychohistory, in particular, offers a root-and-branch challenge to the very fundamentals of historical scholarship. It requires special skills and training, generally in the arcane "science" of psychoanalysis. It also seeks to reorient history toward an understanding of the unconscious emotions underlying the overt actions of human beings as they perform on the stage of history. It claims that traditional history hitherto has mistaken the tip of the iceberg for the great hulking mass of motives, "irrational" rather than rational, that exist beneath the surface of events. Like quantitative historians, psychohistorians redefine what is a document in history, and how it is to be read; they insist that their assertions can only be judged by those versed in the generalizing theories and concepts of psychology, especially psychoanalysis.

How can historians deal with the problems posed by the relative inaccessibility of such an approach to the general student? The answer, I believe, lies in looking at new possibilities, rather than merely new problems. Students today prefer to be activists if given a chance, and lapse into passivity only when all avenues seem closed off to them. Psychohistory offers unusual opportunities for energetic and original participation on the part of students. Applying the concepts and theories of an extra-historical field, students can do their own research in history, emerging with original papers on, say, Eleanor Roosevelt's childhood, or the nature of adolescence in colonial Salem. There is very little a student can do in the beginning stages of traditional history, except take in the received wisdom, even if applying the proverbial critical salt. The situation is dramatically different with the new approaches, and I am sure this is one reason for their spreading popularity.

G.B. Shaw once remarked, "Those who can, do, and those who can't, teach." Witty as it is, Shaw's aphorism is misleading. It hides the fact that some of the best teaching can only take place through doing. Teaching history must be supplemented by students doing history, discovering for themselves how an historical fact becomes a fact and how explanations are constructed.

History is too broad to be encompassed in any one way of teaching. It is too important to be taught in an atmosphere of despair. If we stop worrying so much about our student numbers and concern ourselves more about communicating the traditional strengths of the old approaches and the intellectual vitality of the new approaches, we shall do well enough. With these objectives in mind, practitioners of psychohistory have much to contribute in history classrooms today.

B.M.

Adapted from the **AHA Newsletter** (April, 1976).

The most comprehensive bibliography on psychohistory is Faye Sinofsky, et al., "A Bibliography of Psychohistory," **History of Childhood Quarterly** (Spring, 1975). An excellent critical guide to the literature on psychohistorical methods is William J. Gilmore's "Methodology of Psychohistory: An Annotated Bibliography," **The Psychohistory Review** (September, 1976). A celebrated summons to psychohistorical investigation was issued by William Langer in "The Next Assignment," **American Historical Review** (January, 1958). Recent pronouncements by a variety of scholars include: Frank Manuel, "The Use and Abuse of Psychology in History," **Daedalus** (Winter, 1971); H. Stuart Hughes, "History and Psychoanalysis: The Explanation of Motive," in **History as Art and as Science: Twin Vistas of the Past** (1964); Jacques Barzun, **Clio and the Doctors: Psycho-History, Quanto-History and History** (1974); Bruce Mazlish, "Introduction," **Psychoanalysis and History** (1971); Gerald Izenberg, "Psychohistory and Intellectual History," **History and Theory** (No. 2, 1975); Lloyd DeMause, "The Independence of Psychohistory: A Symposium," **History of Childhood Quarterly** (Fall, 1975). The major journals in the field of psychohistory are **The Psychohistory Review, The Journal of Psychohistory** (formerly the **History of Childhood Quarterly**), and **Psychohistory: The Bulletin of the International Psychohistorical Association.**

FAMOUS HISTORIC FOOTNOTES

The origins of recent experiments with the "workshop" format of history teaching may be traced to a conference on innovation in higher education held at Tufts University in September 1965. The next summer a pilot project at Smith College focused on the possibilities of adapting "laboratory" instruction from the natural sciences to history, and subsequently a group of historians at the University of Wisconsin developed a course that emphasized interpretation of original sources bearing on two or three limited historical topics. The course seemed to work, so variants appeared elsewhere. One was "New Approaches to the Study of History," which began in 1969 at the University of Massachusetts, Amherst, taught by Paul Boyer and Stephen Nissenbaum — the latter having been a graduate student at Wisconsin. Stressing content more than the parent "laboratory" course, Boyer and Nissenbaum prepared case materials that eventually culminated in Salem Possessed *(1974), their award-winning study of early American witchcraft. Other "workshop" topics that they and their colleagues have explored are noted by Nissenbaum below.*

In "New Approaches to the Study of History," we study a single episode all semester, and switch episodes regularly. Various units have been used. Salem witchcraft was the first, back in 1969; another was based on Shays' Rebellion, which took place in the 1780's in Western Massachusetts, where the University of Massachusetts is located; still another unit focuses on the Henry Ward Beecher adultery scandal; and the Lizzie Borden murder case has been taught since 1972. More recently one colleague of mine introduced a unit on the Black Sox scandal of 1919, and just this semester another colleague offered a unit on Jack the Ripper.

What do these episodes have in common? All are very dramatic. They involve either violence or scandal, and sometimes both. (Those are the best.) And they are historically unimporant; if none had happened, little else would have changed. They are just "footnotes" to history. Nevertheless, all are quite famous, almost a part of American folklore. All touched deep nerve endings in the culture in which they took place. Finally, all are quite limited in time, space, and the number of participants. Generally each occurred within a couple of months in a single community. This means that students can learn the *individual people*; in a relatively short period of time they can become deeply familiar, even expert, with actual people and their lives. Personal nitty-gritty, historical trivia — these become relevant here. You get to know people from the past as if they were part of your own family.

The course has a multiple focus. First we want to understand the event itself. But we also want to convey to students a sense of the world in which it took place, and the way real historical forces — which one reads about in history books — actually operated upon and through the event being studied, even though it originally seems to need no broader context whatsoever. Our larger purpose is to give to beginning history students an idea of what historians *do*, instead of simply assigning what they *say*. In this course the students perform the same kinds of operations as professional historians.

Since they are only beginning students, there has to be careful organization and preparation; otherwise the students will simply reach dead ends. In this I have had crucial help from our library staff, and from graduate students at the University, who did most of the legwork to assemble documentary materials. I have even given a graduate seminar in organizing the undergraduate course.

We generally team-teach, Faculty and Teaching Assistants together, because the course takes so much time to plan and because it helps to talk regularly with other people who are teaching it. Our weekly planning sessions become very much a part of our own learning. The course usually enrolls something over 200 students each semester. Although large, it operates primarily in two-hour discussion sections of fifteen to eighteen students apiece. We also have lectures once a week, but the discussion sections are really where the course happens. Almost all the work is based on primary sources. We have no exams, but there are short papers due every few weeks.

The structure of the course is similar with each unit. We start with the event itself, to get acquainted with the people involved and the little details of their world. Then, as naturally as we can, we work outward in space and backward in time, trying to answer questions that have arisen. We try to keep the original event in focus, making our progression to other issues as organic — as unforced — as possible.

S.N.

LIZZIE BORDEN AND HER WORLD

On these two pages, Stephen Nissenbaum describes the approach and findings of his workshop course on Lizzie Borden.

On the hottest day of the summer of 1892, Lizzie Borden of Fall River, Massachusetts, hacked her father and step-mother to death with an axe. This brutal event is the focus of an entire semester's work. What drove Miss Lizzie to commit such an act? In trying to answer this question, we are led deeper and deeper into the inner life of the Borden family, into the history of Fall River, and ultimately into the most basic questions of class structure and sexual politics in the Gilded Age. Most of the initial course reading consists of the rawest kind of data for historical research: trial testimonies, newspaper accounts, city directories, genealogies, probate and business records, and census listings. Later in the semester we turn to other kinds of primary and secondary sources, especially fiction and psychology.

In the first half of the semester we attempt to recapture the personal world of Lizzie Borden. Starting with the murders and the ensuing trial, we then turn to life in the Borden household and the surrounding neighborhood; next we move back in time to study the history of Lizzie Borden's wealthy father, Andrew Jackson Borden. At this point in the course, small groups of students report orally on questions about social mobility in Fall River. We then read *The Rise of Silas Lapham* (1885) by William Dean Howells, which explores some of the difficulties encountered during this period by men of wealth — and their daughters.

Once having established the Borden family in its class context, we return in the second half of the semester to Lizzie Borden herself, using her experiences as a prism through which to view some of the problems faced by American women in the late nineteenth century. Lizzie Borden's brutal crime was clearly not a "typical" act in this or any other period — but what about the frustrations and rage that drove her to commit it? Was she alone in harboring such feelings? Many writers of this period (including Sigmund Freud) commented on the propensity of late nineteenth-century women to nervous and even hysterical behavior. These writers provide an interesting angle from which to view the Lizzie Borden case; and what we know about the Borden case offers an interesting perspective in which to study, and to criticize, these writers.

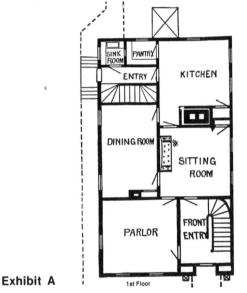

Exhibit A

1st Floor

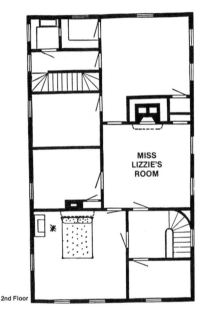

2nd Floor

This is a map of the Borden house, originally drawn to show where the bodies were found. It also provides us with evidence of a very interesting house — which was very much a part of Lizzie Borden's problem. In class we look at this map and talk about it, noticing that on neither the first nor the second floor of the house is there any hall space. To get to any given room, you have to walk through other rooms. That is essentially the way houses were built before the middle of the nineteenth century. It suggests that Lizzie's father, Andrew Jackson Borden, was not particularly concerned to live in a "modern" kind of house, which might have provided privacy for individual members of his family. There are many rooms in the house, so there is privacy to that extent; but there is no sense that people are entitled to be alone in their rooms. If Lizzie wants to get into her own room, she has to go up the stairs and through two other rooms. Andrew Jackson Bordon had the money to buy or build another house, but he stayed put. Perhaps Lizzie did not share her father's lack of concern for privacy.

These are Dun and Bradstreet credit ratings on Andrew Jackson Borden, 1852-1872. An undergraduate in the course found them in the Baker Library at the Harvard Business School. Andrew Jackson Borden was a very rich man, but it turns out he was only a distant kinsman of the prominent Borden family that had developed Fall River from a small farming community in the early nineteenth century into the major textile producing center that it became by the Civil War. Andrew Jackson Borden had been born very poor; he was a self-made man. His rise had nothing to do with textiles. Borden and his partner began as people with good reputation, sound and promising, but obviously with just a modest supply of capital. Borden made his money first as an undertaker; then he went into real estate. You can see him getting richer here.

Exhibit B

Dec. 8, 1852: "We are well acquainted with both these men and consider them good. They have been in business together some eight years and have always maintained a good reputation. Both have families and appear good for wants."

Oct. 13, 1853: "Good for wants."

March 13, 1854: "Young and good businessmen, attentive and industrious, think means sufficient for the business, in good grade and standing here and considered good for their engagements: making money."

Sept. 1, 1854 through July 1, 1855: "Same."

Jan. 1, 1856: "Good for all wants."

July 17, 1856: "Both are rising young men."

Jan. 28, 1863: "Safe and sound."

Aug. 14, 1863: "Doing well and should pay promptly."

Sept. 8, 1866: "Have just bought real estate for $4,000 in good location. Firm among the best."

Feb. 26, 1867: "Getting rich, own $10,000 worth of real estate in the best parts of the city. Sound as a dollar. Doing good business worth $40,000-50,000, good for wants."

Aug. 3, 1867: "Worth at least $60,000."

April 23, 1868: "Good enough they buy for cash."

Oct. 22, 1868: "Doing good business and gaining."

March 6, 1869: "Good enough, worth $75,000 sure and in good credit."

Sept. 10, 1869: "Same."

March 3, 1870: "Good honest and reliable men doing sound business, worth nearly $60,000-70,000, own real estate worth about $50,000, are good and sound."

Sept. 14, 1870: "Doing good business and are good for all wants."

March 8, 1871: "Are safe and reliable, doing a large business, worth $75,000-100,000, and gaining all the time. Perfectly sound."

March 18, 1872: Worth $100,000-125,000, sound and substantial."

Sept. 7, 1872: "Means large, doing well, and in excellent standing."

Dun and Bradstreet Credit Reports on Andrew Jackson Borden and His Partner

This 1892 street list shows the neighborhood of the Borden house. Students quite naturally assume that Andrew Jackson Borden lived in a very rich neighborhood, but we learn here that it was a street of boarding houses, artisans, etc. Borden was clearly the wealthiest person on the block, and could have lived elsewhere. We send the students into the manuscript census to find and examine contrasting upper-class neighborhoods. One of these — a section of Fall River known as "The Hill" — included many fine houses occupied by Bordens. Here was the real Fall River industrial aristocracy. These Bordens sent their children to college, collected art, and engaged in civic philanthropy. Andrew Jackson Borden, born a poor man in 1822, had never participated in this upper-class world. But his daughter Lizzie, born in 1860, grew up after her father had become rich. Did she feel entitled to the modern lifestyle of the upper-class Bordens? Was her crime a tragedy of upward mobility — of "making it" — in late nineteenth-century America?

Exhibit C

WARD 4,B   SECOND STREET

No.	Name	Age	Occup'n.
89	Doughlas, Oscar F.	48	Photographer
89	Paltz, Harold	25	Clerk
89	Young, Frank M.	42	Paver
89	Burton, Austin L.	25	"
89	Robinson, Frank M.	21	"
89	" Alfred	25	"
89	Dowd, Andrew	41	Foreman
89	Welch, Thomas	51	Paver
89	Simmons, Charles	23	Clerk
89	Austin, Anson G.	25	"
89	Deloiry, James	21	Laborer
89	Finney, John	50	Peddler
89	Condon, John	36	Machinist
90	Hamilton, Charles	54	Decorator
90	" Elmer	20	"
90	Gormley, John H.	32	Butcher
91	Bowen, Seabury W.	42	Physician
92	Borden, Andrew J.	67	Retired Mer.
93	Miller, Southard H.	80	Carpenter
93	" Franklin H.	43	Artist
96	Kelley, Michael	35	Physician
98	Chace, Nathan	64	Driver
98	" David	29	Clerk
98	" Mark	54	Hostler
100	Lee, Chew	36	Laundryman
100	Sing, Yenk	39	"
104	Hughes Christopher	52	Clergyman
104	O'Keefe, John D.	30	"
104	Sheedy, David F.	27	"
106	Brennan, George H.	27	Editor
110	Kelly, George H.	48	Restauranteur
110	Whitehead, Edward	61	Clerk
110	Barry, Patrick	31	Tailor
110	Creeden, Edward	31	"
110	Rouke, William	30	Clerk
110	Pike, Nathan	55	Stonemason
116	Robinson, John	54	Confectioner
120	Lee, Hop	53	Laundryman
120	Airlie, Gardner	31	Clerk

SIMULATING THE PAST

William O. Kellogg teaches educational theory and anthropology as well as history at St. Paul's School in Concord, New Hampshire. Below, he discusses his experience running historical simulations in the classroom.

"Simulation" and "gaming" and "role-playing" have become popular terms in the social sciences. A "simulation" tries to capture the essence of a real life situation without the full reality; "games" or "gaming" focus on competitive encounters between human beings; the basic purpose of "role-playing" is to deepen the understanding of social relations by experiencing the actions and feelings of others. Sometimes in the social sciences we carefully separate these three concepts, but frequently they are used together and become interchangeable. Often "simulation" is used to mean all three together.

One assumption underlying simulation also underlies the field of psychohistory. This is that the psychological motivations and complexes that we identify today as basic to human nature — motivations such as the sex drive, aggression, concern for territory, or complexes such as the inferiority complex or Oedipal complex — have been basic to human nature throughout recorded history.

Working from this assumption at St. Paul's, we have developed a role-playing game, or simulation, based upon fifth-century Athens. We began some years ago by asking what our students should know about the Peloponnesian War. To begin with, we decided that students did not need to know all the battles or all the accepted causes of the war. Most important, in our view, was that the war wrecked civilization, as unnecessarily perhaps as World War I. We could tell students this, but felt if

they made the discovery themselves they could understand it much better. We therefore devised for our ninth-grade students the following month-long approach to the history of fifth-century Athens.

For approximately two weeks students investigate the history — political, social, economic, etc. — of Athens, Sparta, or Persia. Students are assigned a country and then divide up the research. One person may thoroughly investigate what it would mean to be a citizen in Athens, while another becomes an expert on Athenian slavery. After the research, during which each group becomes immersed in its society (and in the library), the students spend a week presenting to the rest of the class the information they have found concerning the basic values and goals of their society. Such background data is necessary for any successful simulation.

After the presentations we have a confrontation in a simulated situation. We give students a scenario that summarizes actual events up to 432 B.C., emphasizing the tensions and actions that led to the Peloponnesian War. Some of this material is taken directly from Thucydides, so students are exposed to that great historian. Within each of the three nations, Athens, Sparta, and Persia, roles are assigned depending on each student's individual research; in Athens, for example, one student will represent Pericles, another a slave, etc. Just before the beginning of the simulation, each nation much write down a set of national goals to be achieved during the simulation period. We suggest the goals be achieved without bloodshed, but since this does not seem to be in keeping with Greek attitudes we do not stress the point. To begin the game itself, a move is made by the Control Team. Control keeps the game moving and also makes certain that moves are within the

context of reality, as Control understands it. (The teacher should be designated as the *final* arbiter of actions, or "Zeus." In addition to ultimate control in determining the rationality of all messages, "Zeus" has the power to end the simulation, and the right to introduce "acts of God" — arbitrary actions to force more careful analysis of issues by the participants.) The first move by Control should be a surprise to all the

Guide to Simulations

Among publications available to help teachers plan simulations for their own classes are Ray Glazier, **How to Design Educational Games** (6th ed., 1976); Harold Gorvine, "Teaching History through Role Playing," **The History Teacher** (February, 1970); Michael Inbar and Clarice Stoll, **Simulation and Gaming in Social Science** (1972); and William Nesbitt, **Simulation Games for the Social Studies Classroom** (2nd ed., 1971). Other titles are listed in Cheryl Charles and Ronald Stadsklev, eds., **Learning with Games** (1973), and Cathy Greenblat, "Gaming and Simulation in the Social Sciences: A Guide to the Literature," **Simulation and Games** (December, 1972).

Many commercially packaged games have been produced for use in history classrooms. Denoyer-Geppert Publishers (5235 Ravenswood Avenue, Chicago, Illinois 60611) distribute two popular games: "Armada"and "Empire." Games Central at Abt Associates, Inc. (55 Wheeler Street, Cambridge, Massachusetts 02138), produces and distributes a number of history-related games. For names and descriptions of other commercial games, see either of two comprehensive directories: Charles and Stadsklev, cited above, or David Zuckerman and Robert Horn, **The Guide to Simulations/Games for Education and Training** (3rd ed., 1976).

participants, perhaps a revolt of the Spartan Helots or a failure of the Athenian grape harvest. Various nations then respond by writing their reactions on message forms and sending them through Control to the

other city states. Several years ago one of my students computerized the game period following the crisis introduced by Control. Now all messages go through a computerized Control, which keeps the simulation moving at a very rapid pace.

The debriefing that follows is the essential part of this or any effective simulation. What do the students learn? First, naturally, there is concern as to who won. As you and the class struggle with the hard issue of who won a totally destructive war, parallels with the wars of this century can be raised. A second point that always emerges in the debriefing is how quickly involved and committed to a society one can become when the element of competition is present. If the teacher has assigned certain roles (such as Pericles) to students with the right temperaments, further observations about ego and pride and authority can come to light. Another matter usually mentioned is the difficulty of making decisions under pressure. I like to make the Persian team smaller than the others, and appoint as King an authoritarian type of student; Persian decisions are thus made quickly and easily, as they probably were in a monarchy. On the other hand, the Athenian team labors to make decisions democratically, until — if Pericles plays his role well — he or she takes charge. Students are then led to question what we really mean by Athenian democracy, or any democracy. Other subjects that can be developed from this simulation exercise, depending on the way it is presented and on the research of the students, include the reasons for the failure of a society to resolve conflict through compromise, the meaning of nationalism, and the process by which individuals or societies establish their identities. The last subject is very close to the concerns of the

British Museum

Athenian Orator

psychohistorian.

We have used this simulation for ten years, having begun with the concept of Inter-National Simulation, or Simulex, which was developed at the University of New Hampshire to simulate current international crises. Simulex provided us with what is referred to as a "frame," in the terminology of gaming, and this we applied to a past crisis. Other historical situations have proven adaptable to this kind of exercise, too. It has been our experience that commercially available simulations are usually not structured to meet our needs or to reach the intellectual level of our students, so mostly we have designed our own.

It takes time to create these exercises and often they do not work well at the outset, but any teacher can do it. I suggest that even if you belong in the traditionalist camp of educational theorists, there is a place in your teaching for simuations.

W.O.K.

DIPLOMATIC ROLE-PLAYING

Eugene Lubot, formerly of Wheaton College and now at the University of Tennessee at Chatanooga, has developed a variety of simulations to make Asian history more accessible to American students. One, on the liberation of women in a Chinese village, is described in "History from the Bottom Up"; below he explains how his students recreate negotiations preceding the Opium War.

How do I go about designing a simulation? I have found one useful approach is to zero in on an important but manageable area of controversy. Students play different roles or participate on teams representing different points of view. I have the teams formulate their own strategies (this requires debate within the team); then they must negotiate, through written messages or face-to-face, to resolve the conflict.

British official

National Galleries of Scotland

My simulation of the Opium War negotiations began with the British transmitting a polite but firm memorandum demanding a long list of concessions from the Chinese, including an end to the Canton system, compensation for the opium destroyed, the opening of treaty ports, and an apology to Queen Victoria. The Chinese, relying on the policy of delay and obfuscation they were to follow through the simulation, arrived at the opening session without any statement of their position. They claimed to have misunderstood the directions! Both teams then retired to their separate strategy rooms, and a series of messages were exchanged. The British tried cajolery, threats, and various bargaining packages. The Chinese steadfastly deflected the British approaches, searching for loopholes or contradictions in British messages and refusing to come to grips with the issues being raised.

The students very quickly assumed the attitudes appropriate to their roles. At the first meeting the British behaved in a strident and somewhat crude manner. The Chinese were shocked and felt contempt for them. Some of the British began with sympathy for the Chinese, but their attitudes hardened as the Chinese stalled. They grew more callous, anxious to put the Chinese in their place and to wipe the self-righteous look off their faces.

For all concerned the five hours of the simulation passed quickly. The Chinese eventually offered some concessions, but they were considered inadequate by the British. Finally the British attacked Canton, Shanghai, and ultimately Peking. The Chinese team struggled frantically to survive to the end of the five-hour period. They tried various approaches, such as threatening to cut off all trade and bringing up the issue of the Chinese villager killed by British sailors in 1839. As they ran out of gambits and the

British pressure intensified, the Chinese grew more anxious. They trembled at every knock on the door, sensing impending doom. The British, on the other hand, also felt time slipping away as they worked to obtain a treaty. At the final bell the simulation ended in an impasse, which was probably fortunate since each side could claim a partial victory. The Chinese had been ingenious enough to stave off a treaty, but the British had captured Peking and the Emperor was in flight.

This simulation took place within an historical setting, with basic background information provided. But students did not have to follow a script. They were invited to act creatively, so long as their actions were within the character of their roles and might have happened. This approach may sometimes produce surprises, and you run some risks, but the results are worth it.

E.L.

Adapted from **The History Teacher** (February, 1976).

Chinese official

National Army Museum, London

ROLE-PLAYING AND MORAL DEVELOPMENT

Thomas J. Ladenburg, Coordinator of the Brookline Center in Moral and Developmental Education and a Social Studies teacher at Brookline High School, suggests below how moral reasoning can be taught through historical role-playing.

The great contribution of Lawrence Kohlberg to developmental education was his discovery that educational interventions could stimulate the development of moral reasoning. Historical subject matter can be combined with developmental education in ways that allow cognitive development and moral reasoning to be means of teaching the discipline as well as ends in themselves. A well-conceived historical role-playing exercise is an excellent method for combining these goals.

A complex historical dilemma, drawn from actual case material, can easily be made the basis for a two- or three-day activity and involve many of the thinking and reasoning skills necessary to the learning of history. For example, students can be given the information to stage a mock trial of the British soldiers accused of murder in the Boston Massacre. During the trial, youngsters may act out the parts of witnesses, defendants, lawyers, judges, or "impartial" jurors. The decisions rendered will most likely depend on the skill of opposing lawyers in presenting the case. In the process of preparing opening statements, cross-examination, and summation, students will learn a great deal about our advocacy system of justice. Jurists and witnesses, too, can learn much about courtroom procedure and are required to think through some complex legal issues.

The enterprising teacher can build this lesson on the Boston Massacre into a dilemma mini-unit. He or she could follow

Bernice Donald
"Bern"
   Chorus 1, 2, 3; G.A.A. 1, 2; Girls' Club 1, 2; Pep Club; . . . Ambition: to be a private secretary . . . Likes ice skating and dancing . . . "But your bait!" . . . Favorite Music: Rock 'n Roll . . . Hank Holler.

Franklin May
"Frank"
   Rifle Club 1, 2; Hi-Y 1; . . . Aim: to be a Marine . . . Favorite Food: lobster . . . Pet Peeve: people who think they're Supreme Beings . . . Pastime: seeing Alice . . . Likes boxing.

Stephanie Fleming
"Steph"
   Chorus 1; Girls' Club 1, 2; G.A.A. 1, 2; Pep Club; . . . Ambition: office work . . . Food Choice: fried chicken . . . Favorite Place: drive-in . . . Likes all kinds of pop music . . . Danny.

the mock trial with a reading on the Kent State incident and ask who were the people more clearly to blame, the British soldiers or the National Guardsmen. This discussion may be continued, using the Battle of Lexington as another example; students could examine the militia's stand on the Green, the shot from an unknown source, and the subsequent killings of New England farmers as a parallel case to the Boston Massacre and Kent State discussions. These three lessons would form the basis of the mini-unit and would undoubtedly evoke controversy, hard thinking, and a search for some general principles regarding dissent and protest.

By this time, the students should be immersed in history as process, making decisions they will later stand away from and try to analyze. The reasoning needed to engage in these dilemmas must of necessity become interlaced with a consideration

Whatever happened to the class of 1957?

How have the values of high school students changed over the last twenty years? What do these personal profiles reveal about the relationship of the individual students to the school community? Students can be challenged to consider these and other questions when presented with old high school or college yearbooks.

of the historical factors that played a role in each decision.

T.J.L.

Adapted from the **History Teacher** (February, 1976).

The Brookline Center in Moral and Developmental Education, sponsored by the Danforth Foundation, offers materials such as those cited above and presents workshops for teachers interested in integrating moral and developmental concepts into their curricula. For further information, contact the Center at Brookline High School, 115 Greenough Street, Brookline, Massachusetts 02146.

HISTORICAL PLAY-READING

Reading a period play in class may do more than recreate the atmosphere of the past. If a play is known to have been popular, among amateur as well as professional theatrical groups, it may serve as evidence of how some historical actors role-played in their own time.

Joseph Addison's heroic tragedy *Cato* (1713) is a case in point. Through this play, Cato the younger became a cult figure to the Founding Fathers, living vividly in American minds as a martyr for the cause of liberty. "The post of honor is a private station," says Addison's Cato — and so too, again and again, said patriots like George Mason and George Washington. (Addison's Cato also exclaims over the body of his son, fallen in battle — "What pity is it/That we can die but once to serve our country." Whether Nathan Hale actually uttered similar words, however, is doubtful.) Reduced in length, *Cato* will sustain an animated class that helps to expose the psychological mainsprings of the American Revolutionary movement. It reveals a role that appealed powerfully to political leaders in eighteenth-century America.

TIPS FOR CLASSROOM DIRECTORS

Remember: Reading a play is very different from staging one. It requires less concentration of the players, but more of the audience.

1. Less is more. To minimize tedium, be ruthless in cutting your script in advance. Reverence for the original text is out of place here.
2. Type-cast not by physical appearance but by voice. Try to reserve leading roles for students with sufficient self-confidence to interpret them broadly — even to risk looking foolish.
3. No rehearsal is necessary. At least a day ahead of time, simply give each player a script with his or her part underlined or marked in color and briefly characterized in an accompanying note.
4. If your class is large enough to provide an audience as well as readers, take care to label different characters clearly. Without costumes and movement, people are hard to sort out. It may be helpful to provide name placards, and to distribute an annotated list of dramatis personae.
5. Remember chairs. Otherwise, if you have an old classroom with fixed seats, it will be impossible to arrange your cast up front.
6. Read stage directions and minor parts yourself. This gives you the opportunity not only to keep the play moving at a brisk pace but to offer occasional editorial commentary.

Stephen Botein
Michigan State University
(formerly Harvard University)

Cato contemplating suicide, from an early edition of the play

---

HISTORY AS STORYTELLING

On the night of 28 November we left the Strait and sailed into the great black sea that was to be called Pacific. Magellan and Barbosa wept for joy and fell to their knees rejoicing, but I for my part was on the rear of the ship and looked into the heavens. The stars looked like a sailor captain holding the universe together. And then I knew that only someone with Magellan's strength could have held us all together. He had found the strait that links Atlantic to Pacific.

FERDIN · MAGELLANVS · SVPERATI
ANTARTIC ' FRETI · ANGVS
TIIS · CLARISS·

Thus, in the person of a volunteer mariner named Antonio Pigafetta, Jay O'Callahan recreates the inner drama of Magellan's voyage around the world in 1520-1521. Drawing material from Pigafetta's journal and other surviving documents, O'Callahan has written a story that fills some 45 minutes of one-man theater. For further information about this and other stories that O'Callahan tells at schools, colleges, and libraries, write 90 Old Mount Skirgo Road, Marshfield, Massachusetts 02050.

PERSONALITY AND FILM

Since World War I the medium of film has both enhanced and recorded the dimensions of charismatic political personality. Documentaries of various modern politicians are available at low cost from such university film services as Iowa and Illinois. In addition, it is sometimes possible to identify and rent fictional feature films that have themselves functioned to shape public images and memories of particular national leaders.

> . . . all the signs today point to the fact that a new creed, which can reconcile itself to the facts of human organization, is about to be born. It as yet has no formulas. It is represented vaguely by the personality of Roosevelt who has become a symbol for a political attitude which cannot yet be put into words.
> — Thurman Arnold, **The Folklore of Capitalism** (1937)

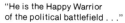

"He is the Happy Warrior
of the political battlefield . . ."

Ralph Bellamy as FDR at the 1924 Democratic Convention
("Sunrise at Campobello," 1960)

History from the Bottom Up

introduction

As early as 1940 Caroline Ware urged the exploration of "history from the bottom up," but only in the past ten years have many American historians — using new techniques and new sources — begun seriously to follow this advice. Numerous recent studies concentrate on the common people so easily forgotten in conventional histories that rely on more immediately accessible records to reproduce the experience of "great white men."

For some historians, "history from the bottom up" implies more than the need to study workers, peasants, women, Blacks, or immigrants; it also implies the need to alter our angle of vision, to stop looking at the past from the perspective of successful, powerful elites and to start looking at the past from the viewpoint of the oppressed and exploited. This is the approach of the English historian E.P. Thompson, who has sought "to rescue the poor stockinger, the Luddite cropper, the 'obsolete' handloom weaver, the 'utopian' artisan, and even the deluded follower of Joanna Southcott, from the enormous condescension of posterity."

The "enormous condescension" of much traditional scholarship has often influenced history teaching as well. As a result of this bias, the content of conventional history courses may be foreign to the experience of many students, and therefore perhaps abstract, unreal, ultimately unimportant.

As it happens, many teachers in the New England region have lately begun to teach history from new perspectives. As with scholarship, so with teaching: "history from the bottom up" approaches new subjects with new methods. In adding previously neglected groups to history curricula, history teachers have also reshaped the conceptual frameworks of their courses. The history of the American working class, for example, cannot be organized around changing presidential administrations. For some teachers, too, the history of common people should not be taught from a neutral detached stance; it is necessary to involve students directly with their own past, and to encourage the formulation of committed opinion.

Appropriately, as a glance at the institutional affiliations of contributors will indicate, this is a broadly based movement in history teaching that draws on many sources besides university scholarship. Indeed, it is quite apparent that some New England teachers have anticipated that scholarship in their classrooms, and — in collaboration with students — have begun to generate significant research materials of their own.

". . . and so the poor peasant's daughter liquidated the handsome young prince, set up a people's government, and lived happily ever after."

Drawing by Chas. Addams, © 1945, 1973. **The New Yorker Magazine, Inc.**

THE AFRICAN EXPERIENCE

Until lately, African history was taught as little more than a footnote to European history. The main themes were the extension of European control over the continent and resulting rivalries among the colonial powers. Throughout most of this story Africans themselves were treated as a faceless mass with only a small supporting role in the final chapter — in which the European powers gave up their African empires.

Recent changes in political power, however, have undermined the European-centered structure of this subject matter. African history is increasingly being taught from the perspective of Africans — and all Africans at that, not just their leaders. African history courses no longer begin with the arrival of Europeans on the continent, but instead trace the evolution of indigenous social patterns, cultural practices, and political forms.

Reproduced below is the syllabus of Hatim M. Amiji's "Introduction to African Civilization" at the University of Massachusetts, Boston. Focusing on the internal dynamics of selected pre-colonial African societies, Amiji considers such themes as the genesis of man in Africa; the cultures of gatherers and hunters; the civilizations of the Nile Valley; the rise and fall of the Kingdoms of Ghana, Mali, Songhai, and the city states of East Africa; the development of the slave trade and its impact on African societies; and African art and religion.

Introduction to African Civilization

I. INTRODUCTION: PRE-COLONIAL AFRICA
— THE MYTH AND THE REALITY

Film: **The African Continent**

II. FOUNDATIONS OF AFRICAN SOCIETY

Chinua Achebe, **Things Fall Apart** (1959), pp. 7-125.

III. AFRICAN PRE-HISTORY: MIGRATIONS AND POPULATION MOVEMENTS

Ulli Beier, ed., "Revolt Against God — A Fang Creation Myth," **The Origin of Life and Death: African Creation Myths** (1966).
Merrick Posnansky, "Cave Keeping 20,000 B.C.," in **Prelude to East African History** (1966).
Edward Weyer, Jr., "Hunters and Gatherers: The Bushmen," in **Primitive Peoples Today** (1959).
Film: **The Hadza of Central Tanzania.**

IV. EGYPT IN ANCIENT AFRICA

Robert O. Collins, ed., **Problems in African History** (1968), pp. 10-28.
Lionel Casson and the Editors of Time-Life Books, "Gods and the Afterlife," in **Ancient Egypt** (1965).
W.E.B. DuBois, **The World and Africa** (1947), pp. 98-114.

V. THE EMPIRE OF GHANA

Basil Davidson, **A History of West Africa** (1967), pp. 24-51.
Edward W. Bovill, "The Gold of Ghana and Wangara," in **The Golden Trade of the Moors** (1958).
"The Word of God," **The Koran.**

VI. THE EMPIRE OF MALI

Davidson, **History of West Africa**, pp. 53-63.
Djibril T. Niane, **Sundiata: An Epic of Old Mali** (1965).

VII. SONGHAI AND THE "GOLDEN AGE" OF AFRICAN HISTORY

Davidson, **History of West Africa**, pp. 65-72, 119-129, 149-191.

VIII. THE STATES OF EAST AFRICA

Zoe Marsh and G.W. Kingsnorth, "Swahili Cities and the Coast of East Africa," in **An Introduction to the History of East Africa** (1957).
Joao de Barros, "Mines and Fortresses," in Basil Davidson, ed., **The African Past: Chronicles from Antiquity to Modern Times** (1964).
Ibn Battuta, "Kilwa in 1331," in Davidson, ed., **The African Past.**

IX. THE BEGINNINGS OF EUROPEAN ENTERPRISE IN EAST AND WEST AFRICA

Davidson, **History of West Africa**, pp. 197-201.
Basil Davidson, **The African Slave Trade: Pre-Colonial History, 1450-1850** (1961), pp. xiii-xxiii, 3-21.

X. SLAVES AND SLAVING

Davidson, **African Slave Trade**, pp. 21-30, 33-113.

XI. IMPACT OF THE SLAVE TRADE ON AFRICAN SOCIETIES

Davidson, **African Slave Trade**, pp. 117-162, 199-290.

XII. RELIGION, ESTHETICS, AND ART IN PRE-COLONIAL AFRICA

Basil Davidson and the Editors of Time-Life Books, "Gods and Spirits" and "Arts Capture Life," **African Kingdoms** (1966).
Achebe, **Things Fall Apart**, pp. 126-191.

H.M.A.

ORGANIZING ETHNIC GROUP DATA

What is known or not known about ethnic groups in the United States? What can be said? What needs to be said? What information is not available? The following checklist/outline (slightly abridged) was worked out by the editors of the Harvard Encyclopedia of American Ethnic Groups *(now in preparation) as a guide for their thinking and as an aid for their contributors. Not applicable in every particular to the more than 100 groups to be represented in the volume, it was designed to be suggestive rather than prescriptive. Teachers may find it useful for discussions and research projects.*

Origins:
— where did the group originate? nation-state? region? linguistic group? were group members exiles or refugees? a people among peoples? a remnant?

Migration:
— who migrated? how many? who stayed behind? how and why was the migration organized? was it voluntary or involuntary? what policies at point of origin affected migration? at point of arrival?

Arrival:
— did the group arrive over a short or long time? did immigrants come one by one, in small units, or en masse? has the group been continually or sporadically refreshed by new arrivals? has there been return migration? re-immigration?

Settlement:
— what kind of society did the group enter? colonial? frontier? rural and agricultural? urban? industrial? was the pattern of geographical mobility toward dispersion or segregation? from city to country? from city to city?

Economic life:
— what was entry employment? did specialization develop? has there been a characteristic pattern of enterprise?

Family:
— what has been the common family form? kinship ties? marriage patterns? intermarriage? is data available on family size, mortality, divorce?

Culture:
— has the group maintained its original language? orally? in written form? everyday or ceremonial use? what have been characteristic modes of cultural expression? literature? theater? music? dance? art? costume? gastronomy?

Education:
— how has the group been educated, informally as well as formally? is there data on literacy in English? were there parochial alternatives to public education?

Religion:
— has the religious identity of the group been shaped in America or remained continuous with the place of origin? what have been the characteristic forms of religious organization? what have been the characteristic patterns of belief or unbelief?

Social organization:
—what have been the common patterns of association? voluntary societies? religious and political activity? who have been group leaders? how have they emerged or been chosen? from the center or periphery of the group? how have they interacted with the larger society?

Politics:
— to what extent has the group entered local and national political life? what have been characteristic forms of political organization? what has motivated participation? ideology? interest?

Social structure:
— how have class and ethnic identity been related? has stratification within the ethnic group been parallel or incongruous with the system of the larger society? what have been the patterns and sources of social mobility?

Intergroup relations:
— what contacts has the group made with other ethnic groups? what accomodation has been reached with the larger society? acculturation? assimilation? minority status? separation? experiences of racism, prejudice, discrimination?

Group maintenance:
— what resources have been utilized to maintain the boundaries of the ethnic community?

Ann Orlov, Managing Editor

Native Americans

What is the meaning of "immigration" or "bicentennial" (not to mention "massacre"), from a Native American perspective? "Most books about Native Americans have been written by nonIndians," observed members of a Native American Internship Team organized in 1975-1976 by the Children's Museum in Boston. "They present a nonIndian and often degrading view of our culture and people today and of our history." Funded by a grant from the National Endowment for the Humanities, the Team drew up a list of guidelines, suggestions, and resources for approaching Native American studies. These materials emphasize the need to identify stereotypical images of Native Americans not only in books but in the mass media and such commercial merchandise as toys and greeting cards. For further information about this project and other materials relating to Native American history, contact Judy Battat, Children's Museum, Jamaicaway, Boston, Massachusetts 02130.

THE WORLD OF WORK

Below, Martin Sleeper and Shomer Zwelling describe the "World of Work" program they have helped develop at Old Sturbridge Village.

Work is a dominant theme in Old Sturbridge Village's recreation of rural New England in the early nineteenth century. We have developed instructional materials on work for schools as well as museums and other educational agencies. Drawing on the resources of Old Sturbridge Village, these materials provide an important historical and humanistic perspective for understanding work in contemporary society.

"World of Work" raises central questions about work, and its meaning in American society. What is work? Why do people work? What are the gratifications and frustrations of particular job and work situations? What is leisure? Analyzing such questions within a contemporary framework has enhanced our understanding of work in the nineteenth century. Moreover, this orientation is especially useful for students.

> **Other materials available on the World of Work**
>
> Old Sturbridge Village has kits on "Farming Was Family Work" and "From Farm to Factory" that include background discussion of work, edited primary sources, reproductions of nineteenth-century artifacts, prints, slidetapes, learning activities, role cards, and bibiographies. In addition, the museum has produced a 27-minute film on "Working in Rural New England." For further information, write the Museum Education Department, Old Sturbridge Village, Sturbridge, Massachusetts 01506.

Why do your parents work? What do they do in their work? How does their day differ from yours? Asking and answering such questions, students gain an awareness of work in modern society that makes their study of work in history more relevant and meaningful.

For the study of work in the nineteenth century, perhaps the single most important concept to develop is that of industrialization. The phrase "industrial revolution" has been so overworked that one is apt to use the term blithely and ignore its momentous implications. Industrialization at its most fundamental level, however, involved not only a change in the work process, but a major re-orientation in the worker's life, family, and community.

One significant theme of "World of Work" concerns the ways young people choose careers — a subject especially relevant to adolescent education. On the opposite page is a letter written by Sally Rice, a young cotton mill worker in early nineteenth-century New England. A classroom lesson analyzing this letter might begin with an examination of the farm as a work environment, using farm diaries of the period and slides of farm work at Old Sturbridge Village. Farm and factory work can then be compared in terms of work schedules, work spaces, and the role of the family as a work unit. This exercise should make the choice of working on the farm or in the mill that confronted Sally Rice more meaningful to students. To adolescents the letter might be construed as an issue of occupational choice that faced many young girls of that period. That issue can then be compared to career decisions today. Adolescents might also be asked to talk with their parents about career choices in their lives that involved adventure, risk, or uncertainty, and then chart the parents' work history noting points where crucial decisions were made. Generational conflict is suggested in the letter, for Sally acknowledges her father's opposition to her going into the mill, and her description of her religious experience might be seen in part as her attempt to ease her father's concern and her own sense of guilt. Contemporary adolescents are likely to recognize this inter-generational tension, and this aspect of the letter can lead to an important discussion relating family pressure and occupational choice.

Several learning activities for younger students can also be structured around this letter as well. Using related sources from the period, children can build a hypothetical model of the factory in which Sally worked. The model can be supplemented with pictures and diagrams of mill machines and excerpts from a mill agent's diary, to give students a picture of Sally's work environment. Using the wage rates in the letter, and her account of her production and her expenses, children can construct a hypothetical weekly budget for Sally. These activities can then be the basis for role-playing several hypothetical incidents involving Sally, her parents, and her fellow workers.

M.S.
S.Z.

At the age of seventeen, Sally Rice left the small Vermont farm on which she had been raised to strike out on her own. After working for a few years as a hired girl on a farm, she went to work in the Masonville cotton mill in Thompson, Connecticut.

Dear Father:

Masonville, Sunday, February 23, 1845

I now take my pen in hand to let you know where I am and how I came here and how my health is. I have been waiting perhaps longer than I ought to without letting you know where I am and yet I had a reason for so doing. Well knowing that you were dolefully prejudiced against a cotton factory, and being no less prejudiced myself, I thought it best to wait and see how I prospered and also whether I was going to stay or not. I well knew that if I could not make more in the mill than I can doing housework I should not stay. Now I will tell you how I happened to come. The Saturday after New Years I came to Masonville in Thompson, Connecticut, with James Alger to visit his sister who weaves in the mill. We came Saturday and returned to Millbury on Monday. While here I was asked to come back and learn to weave. I did not fall in with the idea at all because I well knew that I should not like it as well as housework and knowing that you would not approve of my working in the mill. But when I considered that I had got myself to take care of, I knew I ought to do that way I can make the most and save the most. I concluded to come and try, promising Mrs. Waters that if I did not like it I would return the first of April.

I have wove 4 weeks and have wove 6.89 yds. We have one dollar and .10 cents for a hundred yards. I wove with Oliver Alger one week to learn and I took 2 looms 2 weeks and now I have 3 looms. I get along as well as anyone could expect. I think that very likely before the year is out I shall be able to tend 4 looms and then I can make more. O. and P. Alger make three dollars a week besides their board. We pay 1.25 for our board. We three girls board with a Widow Whitemore. She is a first rate homespun woman. I like it quite as well as I expected but not as well as housework. To be sure it is a noisy place and we are confined more than I like to be. I do not wear out my clothes and shoes as I do when I do housework. If I can make 2 dollars per week besides my board and save my clothes and shoes I think it will be better than to do housework for nine shillings. I mean for a year or two. I should not want to spend my days in a mill unless they are short because I like a farm too well for that. My health is good now. And I say now that if it does not agree with my health I shall give it up at once. I consider if my health is gone I am done at once. I have been blessed with good health always ever since I began to work out. I have not been confined to my bed but one day since I was sick with mumps the time Grandmother Rice died. I was very sick one day when I was at Mrs. Waters.

Dear Father, in my last letter I told you I had morally reformed. Yes I trust I have and bless God that he unsealed my eyes to see where I was standing, and where I have been since I became a backslider. The name haunts me. It all seems like a dream. Pray for me, Father, that if I ever enjoyed Religion I may enjoy it again and do as much good as I have hurt in the cause and the great God assisting me I will try to pray for myself. I feel I am perfectly willing to give up all into the hands of God and will try to lead a better life than I have done.

I want you to write as soon as you get this. Address your letter to Masonville, Thompson, Connecticut. Give my love to Mother & to all our folks. Tell Brother to write. I have not written to Hiram yet. I want to know where Ephraim is and how you all do Father.

Good bye
Sarah Rice

INDUSTRIALIZATION IN AMERICA

Larry Bucciarelli and Michael Folsom, of M.I.T., have developed a course that explores the meaning of American industrialization and its impact on culture and technology. A brief outline follows their description.

Our first three classes familiarize participants with each other and with some of the issues of the course. We try to find out where each of us is starting from in our attitudes and understanding of things like history, labor, and technology. We examine both the different perspectives that scholars bring to the study of these things and what they mean in our own lives.

The group of classes and field trips on the New England Textile Mill is the heart and focus of the course. These field trips take us to Old Sturbridge Village, the Slater Mill Museum, Rhode Island mill villages, the Merrimack Valley Textile Museum, the Lowell Historical Museum, the Isabella Stuart Gardner Museum, and the dams, canals, and factories of Lowell. We visit these sites not because the textile industry is the most "romantic" or important we might study, but for two reasons: one accidental, one necessary and compelling. We are interested in this process of industrialization — that is, the change of an economy, a culture, a productive system based on agriculture and hand craft to one based on machinery. The textile industry of New England in the first half of the nineteenth century is where and when that process started in this nation. This is the necessary reason for our course. The accidental reason is obvious: New England is where we happen to be. A primary

aspect of this course is its integration of field experience into the curriculum. We believe that one cannot comprehend the history of industrial technology without encountering its works, and the mill towns of New England are close at hand for us to study.

One of the peculiarities of the Industrial Revolution is that, unlike many other developments in human history, it did not engender a wealth of serious imaginative literature to explore, celebrate, dissect, and confirm its own significance. This in itself is a crucial commentary on the nature of industrialization. There are some exceptions, however — several key works of great literary value, in which we can see major nineteenth-century American writers grappling in their own terms with the images and issues presented to the nation by the ascendance of industrial technology. Four classes on nineteenth-century literature pro-

vide a distinct change of pace, and perhaps a disturbing shift in perspective.

A very brief look at the development of the American steel industry in the later nineteenth century complements the earlier discussion of the textile industry, the real focus of the course. We search for suggestions of similarity and contrast between two major examples of the process of industrialization. Are certain phenomena essential to the nature of industrialization? Or have they to do with accidental characteristics of a particular product or the special features of a particular age and community?

L.B.
M.F.

A Connecticut Hat Factory in the 1830's

Lowell Textile Mill

Culture and Technology in America:
The Industrial Revolution

Introduction (3 classes)

Industrialization I: The New England Textile
  Mill
  The Agrarian Background (2 classes, 1 field
    trip)
  The Mill Village (1 field trip)
  Ideologies and Origins of Manufacturing
    (1 class)
  The Lowell Experiment (7 classes, 1 field
    trip)
    Engineering
    Economics
    People

Culture
Exploitation and Protest
Maturity and Decline (2 classes, 1 field trip)

Industrialization II: Visions and Nightmares
  in Nineteenth-Century Literature (4 classes)

Industrialization III: The Steel Mill (3 classes)
  Engineering
  Motives and Methods of Social and
    Economic Organization
  Life in the Steel Mill Town

Conclusions (3 classes, 1 field trip)
  The Culture and Consequences of
    Nineteenth-Century Industrialization

Factory Visits

You and your class can see Indian corn ground into cornmeal at Kenyon's 1886 Grist Mill in Usquepaugh, Rhode Island; watch the production of thread at the American Thread Company in Willimantic, Connecticut; or visit an automobile assembly line at the General Motors Plant in Framingham, Massachusetts. These and other industrial tours are listed in the American Automobile Association's tour books of the New England states and in **U.S.A. Plant Visits, 1977-1978** (Superintendent of Documents, Government Printing Office, Washington ,D.C. 20402).

WHAT DO THESE PICTURES TELL YOU ABOUT THE RELATION BETWEEN PEOPLE AND THEIR WORK?
HOW DID WORK AFFECT THE COMMUNITY?

Homestead, Pennsylvania

Lewis W. Hine

WORKING PEOPLE

BOSTON'S WORKERS: A LABOR HISTORY

As part of the Boston Public Library's "Learning Library Program," funded by the National Endowment for the Humanities, James Green of the University of Massachusetts at Boston (College of Community and Public Service) taught a course in the Spring of 1977 on the history of the Boston working class. The course attracted a diverse audience of college students, trade unionists, and other interested Bostonians. The Boston Public Library will publish the lectures in 1978 as a paperback book designed for high school and college use. Contact the Library for further information.

This lecture series attempted to show some of the ways in which Boston's working people have made their own history in the past 200 years. In the recent Bicentennial celebrations, the public heard much about the great white fathers of the American Revolution; but, with the exception of Paul Revere, little was said of the artisans, farmers, and laborers who were the foot soldiers of the war against British tyranny. Boston also toasted its great nineteenth-century businessmen, politicians, reformers, and literary lights, but few toasts were raised to the working people who created the businessmen's wealth, elected the politicians to office, and served as the subjects of studies by reformers and artists.

Among the Bostonians examined in the lectures were the Yankee artisans who carried Revolutionary ideals into the industrial revolution; the Irish and Italian laborers who literally built the city of Boston in its modern form; the Yankee "farm girls" who staffed the offices, stores and school rooms; the Irish and Afro-American women who performed domestic chores for the city's elite; and the Jewish and Italian "working girls" who kept the sewing machines humming in Boston's garment lofts.

These working people not only contributed to the city economically; they also made important social, cultural, and political contributions to Boston's history. By examining their contributions, it is possible to see the limits of the traditional historical view of the worker as "economic man," concerned only with "bread and butter" matters.

The lecture series also tried to contest the view that workers have been "helpless victims" in history, dominated by the Brahmin elite, manipulated by demagogic politicians, depressed by slum life, crushed by the "juggernaut" of capital. This passive view of workers is mistaken. On the other hand, the lectures also considered why the majority of the city's population has failed through various means (legislative reform, trade unions, "workingmen's parties," etc.), to take control of its own fate. Boston's workers have made their own history, but they have done so within the limits imposed by the capitalist economy in which they worked and the competitive society in which they lived.

J.G.

SOURCES FOR TEACHING THE HISTORY OF WORKING PEOPLE

Paul Faler teaches the history of working people at the University of Massachusetts at Boston.

For a people once said to be inarticulate, working people have left a considerable record. Workingmen's newspapers, autobiographies, interviews, letters, poems, and other primary sources are invaluable not just for research but for teaching. As historians we recognize these materials as indispensable for our own understanding of history; the same is true for students. Moreover, students often bring new insight that can be both refreshing and illuminating.

In my labor history course I have used selections from John Commons's *Documentary History of American Industrial Society* (1910-1911); Leon Litwack's *American Labor Movement* (1962); Kenneth Lasson's lengthy *The Workers: Portraits of Nine American Jobholders* (1971); and the Leon Stein and Philip Taft collection of short autobiographies, *Workers Speak* (1971). The oral histories on the 1930's and 1940's in Alice and Staughton Lynd's *Rank and File: Personal Histories by Working Class Organizers* (1973) are excellent. Although many colleagues do not agree, I find

> For more readings, films, and records useful in teaching the history of North American workers, consult Jim O'Brien et al., **Guide to Working Class History** (1976). It is available for 60 cents (plus 30 cents tax and handling) from the New England Free Press, 60 Union Square, Somerville, Massachusetts 02143.

Joseph Howell's *Hard Living on Clay Street* (1973) a good account of cultural conflict within the ranks of working people. I have also used Harriette Arnow's *The Dollmaker* (1954), one of the finest novels published in the last 25 years. These materials help recreate for students the world of working people as they saw and lived it.

For secondary works, I have relied heavily on Herbert Gutman and Gregory Kealey's *Many Pasts* (1973), the best collection in the field. It brings together both articles and excerpts from monographs that would otherwise be difficult to obtain. I cannot, unfortunately, recommend any single outstanding text. As a historian I have many criticisms of Richard Boyer and Herbert Morais's *Labor's Untold Story* (1955), but students have rated it highly for its engaging prose.

My students have both enjoyed and learned from renditions of working class songs by Pete Seeger, Woody Guthrie, and Utah Phillips. On several occasions I have managed to find a student able and willing to give a concert of working class ballads. Philip Foner's recent *American Labor Songs of the Nineteenth Century* (1975) provides selections for almost any purpose.

The Poor and Society

In "The Poor and Society," a seminar given at Bowdoin College, Dan Levine explores ways that various industrializing societies have thought about and attempted to deal with the poor. The course offers materials for a comparison of conditions and developments in Germany, Denmark, Great Britain, and the United States between 1830 and 1930.

Basic requirements include **The Poor Law Report of 1834**, Robert Bremner, **From the Depths** (1956), and Herman Ausubel, **The Late Victorians** (1955).

Also required of each student is a special research project. Using primary sources alone, this paper must examine one of the issues raised during the semester. Suggested topics include the investigation of state poverty institutions in Maine and other states, poverty in Charles Dickens's **Oliver Twist** (1837) and Upton Sinclair's **The Jungle** (1906), and the lot of the poor in Denmark as reflected in Martin Anderson Nexos's **Pelle the Conqueror: Daybreak** (1916).

The amount and quality of visual material is also growing. Despite limitations, *The Inheritance* (1964) is an excellent film, as is *Union Maids* (1976). I have borrowed heavily from M.B. Schnapper's *American Labor: A Pictorial Social History* (1972), using an opaque projector for many of the excellent photographs and graphics he has assembled.

For a number of reasons I try to combine local history with the history of working people. If an overall goal is to explain how things got to be the way they are, then I find we must explain the origins of particular institutions, industries, social relations, and political affiliations that are still strong and familiar to the types of students I teach. Materials for the study of local history are accessible and abundant. For example, I have taught labor history workshops focusing on such key episodes in local working class history as the 1834 Charlestown Convent Fire and the 1863 Boston Draft Riot.

Fortunately, I think we can say there is growing interest in the history of working people, much of it coming from working people themselves. Underlying the study of history is a desire for self-understanding. Many of my students wish to know more about their own history, the origins of traditions, institutions, and ideas that are a part of their world and ours.

P.F.

Labor History On Film

There are many films that can be effectively utilized in labor history courses. Here is a selection of possible films, many of which have been used by James Green and Paul Faler:

Black Fury (1935, UA Sixteen, 729 7th Ave., New York, N.Y., 10015), Hollywood film on labor conflict; **Children of Labor** (1977, CD Film Workshop, 28 Fisher Ave., Boston, Massachusetts 02120), Finish-American radicalism and its repression; **The Emerging Woman** (1975, Film Images, 17 W. 60th St., New York, N.Y. 10023); **Finally Got the News** (1971, Tricontinental Film Center, 333 6th Ave., New York, N.Y. 10014), the League of Revolutionary Black Workers, a group which organized in Detroit auto plants in the late 1960's; **Harlan County, U.S.A.** (1976, Cinema 5, 595 Madison Ave., New York, N.Y. 10009), both contemporary and 1930's coal mining struggles; **The Inheritance** (1964, Amalgamated Clothing Workers' Union), the struggle of immigrant workers to gain union recognition and political power; **Joe Hill** (1971, Films Inc., 733 Greenbay Rd., Wilmette, Illinois 60091), partially fictionalized account of Wobbly troubadour; **Memorial Day Massacre of 1937** (1976, Illinois Labor History Society, 2800 N. Sheridan, Chicago, Illinois 60657); **Native Land** (1942, Highlander Research and Education Center, Box 245A, Rt. 3, New Market, Tennessee 37820), the repression of the labor movement as revealed in testimony taken by the LaFollette Committee of 1938; **Sacco and Vanzetti** (1970, Warner Bros., 400 Warner Blvd., Burbank, California 91505); **Salt of the Earth** (1954, Audio-Brandon Films, 34 MacQuesten Parkway So., Mount Vernon, New York 10550), strike in New Mexico mining town; **Shape of an Era** (1974, CD Film Workshop), Minnesota hardrock miners in the early twentieth century; **Union Maids** (1976, New Day Films, Box 315, Franklin Lakes, New Jersey 07417), militant women labor organizers in the 1930's and 1940's; **United Action Means Victory** (1940, United Auto Workers), on the 1939 GM tool and die strike; **With These Hands** (1970, International Ladies' Garment Workers' Union), about garment work.

ORAL HISTORY

Talking to "old timers" allows students to unearth, preserve, and understand the stories of people sometimes (and mistakenly) labelled "inarticulate." Below and on the opposite page Steven Miller of the Cambridge-Goddard Graduate School for Social Change and Theodore B. Belsky of the American International College Oral History Center suggest how oral history can be used in teaching "history from the bottom up."

LABOR ORAL HISTORY

Even though traditional American mythology denies the existence of class struggle, it is obvious that workers have often been in conflict with their employers. History textbooks are seldom written from the point of view of the worker, much less by workers themselves. Therefore, both to broaden the material I am able to present and to enliven the classroom, I introduce Labor Oral History into my courses. I have found that almost any labor activist — either old or young — can give an interesting talk, but the best presentations come from activists in the "progressive" wing of the union movement: United Electrical Workers, Packinghouse Workers, District 65 of the Distributive Workers of America, Hospital Workers 1199, etc. These people have experience discussing their work analytically and are most willing to consider the shortcomings as well as the achievements of organized labor.

My method of conducting Labor Oral History has been relatively simple. I call the local offices of the unions in which I am interested, explain what I am doing, and ask if they could recommend any present or former labor activists. When I call people whose names I have been given, I make sure to ask if they can make any additional recommendations.

The procedure in the classroom is equally simple. Having read various books about labor history, the students have some idea of the general issues and events about which our guests are to speak. Some talk about their personal experiences; others give more union-oriented or general historical information. The most powerful talks combine personal stories with general statements about broad trends. After each talk we have a period for questions and general discussion.

Other ways to teach the experience of workers would be to have students go out and visit worker activists; to tour a factory with a union guide as well as a company PR official; to invite a member of a picket line to come to class and tell what is going on and why; and to ask the head of the local central labor council to meet with students.

S.M.

Milton Rogovin

A primary objective of the oral history interview is to establish rapport with the respondents.

Oral History Centers

The Oral History Center at American International College makes material available for teachers interested in oral history, including a "Checklist of steps to consider in an oral history project," a one-page statement on "Implications of oral history for the respondent and the community," and examples of forms showing how to preserve and catalogue oral history tapes. For copies of these materials or for additional advice in setting up your own oral history project, contact the Oral History Center, American International College, Springfield, Massachusetts 01109.

Teachers might also like to join the New England Oral History Association. Contact John Fox, Department of History, Salem State College, Salem, Massachusetts 01970.

THEMES FOR ORAL HISTORY PROJECTS

It is important to select and clearly define a theme from the very beginning. A specific topic sets a realistic limit on what shall be done, helps you to select qualified participants for the project, and makes it possible to evaluate its worth. Themes that focus on specific events, people, or community concerns are usually easier to organize and more interesting than general topics. For example, it is better to trace the impact of a shoe factory on a community's economic structure than to review superficially the economic growth of the town.

Below is a list of possible themes for oral history projects:

—Political, social, and economic roles of labor unions within the community.

—Development of local military and veterans' organizations (e.g., National Guard, Volunteer Militia, American Legion).

—Changes in the community's school system through time; schoolboard-community relations; impact of specific teachers, principals, and superintendents on the community, etc.

—Development of significant industries and occupations in the community, from both managerial and employee viewpoints.

—History of ethnic and minority groups and their interrelations with the community; political and social roles of ethnic organizations (e.g., Hibernians, Sons of Italy); effect of immigration on community structure and attitudes.

—History of voluntary associations (e.g., lodges, clubs) in the community.

—History of specific churches and other religious organizations and their roles in the development of the community; impact of religious leaders.

—Outstanding or unusual political events or figures in the community's past; visits of national or international leaders.

—Development and changing roles of political organizations; impact of changes in forms of local government (e.g., from mayoral to city-manager form).

—Impact of disaster on the community (e.g., hurricanes, floods, influenza epidemics, etc.).

—Transportation in the community; impact of the coming of the automobile; replacement of trolleys by buses; discontinuance of railroad service, etc.

—Family life through time; courtship, child-rearing, husband-wife roles, adult-juvenile relations (e.g., the 'generation gap' through time); the impact of radio and television.

—Effect of physical or environmental change on recreation in the community (e.g., the building of a stadium, destruction of a theater or opera house, elimination of parks or woodlands, pollution of local fishing areas, etc.).

— T.B.B.

Oral History Reading List

Good instruction manuals for the neophyte interviewer include Raymond Gordon, **Interviewing: Strategy, Techniques and Tactics** (1969), chapters 2, 3, and 5; Stephen Richardson et al., **Interviewing: Its Forms and Functions** (1965), chapter 3; W.L. Warner and Paul Lunt, **The Social Life of a Modern Community** (1941), pp. 45-53.

Among the classic works of this young field are Studs Terkel, **Hard Times: An Oral History of the Great Depression** (1970); Theodore Rosengarten, **All God's Dangers: The Life of Nate Shaw** (1974); Alice and Staughton Lynd, **Rank and File: Personal Histories by Working Class Organizers** (1973); and John

Niehardt, ed., **Black Elk Speaks** (1932).

William Cutler, "Accuracy in Oral History Interviewing," **Historical Methods Newsletter** (June, 1973), discusses a general methodology. **Red Buffalo** (Nos. 2 and 3, 1972) is a special double issue devoted to oral history, and includes an annotated bibliography by Steven Trimble. The annual **Oral History Review** reports on the latest developments in the field.

HARD TIMES ON TAPE

While teaching at the Worcester Polytechnic Institute, William Mulligan developed a course on "The Shaping of Post-1920 America" that made substantial use of oral history.

The key element in my course was a sequence of two written assignments. For the first, each student was asked to read Studs Terkel, **Hard Times** (1970), and then interview someone who had lived through the Great Depression. In addition to the Terkel book, I put several oral history guides on reserve in the library and provided very detailed instructions. After some initial grumbling, nearly every student developed a degree of enthusiasm; several conducted lengthy, probing interviews. Most said that the exercise had changed their view of the nature of history. The second assignment allowed students to choose among several topics. Most popular was an oral interview with someone who had lived through the 1960's.

W.M.

A BRIEF CHECKLIST FOR THE INTERVIEWER IN ORAL HISTORY

The Interview

1. Where is the tape recorder in relation to the respondent and to you? Is the recorder in good working order? How often is it necessary to "fiddle" with it, and thus increase its visibility to the respondent?

2. Who is doing most of the talking — you or the respondent?

3. Are you continually prompting the respondent? Are you in a hurry?

4. Are **pauses** (yours or the respondent's) causing problems? Is he collecting his thoughts, or is he bored, confused, or threatened?

5. Are you **teaching** or **preaching**, rather than interviewing? Are you allowing the **respondent** to do so, rather than narrating?

6. Are the respondent's answers predominantly of the "yes-no" variety? If this has been true from the beginning of the interview, there is something wrong with your questions. If it begins when you are well into the interview, as is more common, then rapport has been damaged. Either way, take a break at this point. Monosyllabic answers are usually a sign of trouble. If they occur often at this stage in the interview, then fatigue or anxiety are likely causes. It is then time for "fence-mending."

7. Are you using **probe** questions effectively? A probe question has two major functions:

A. Overcoming respondent resistance in sensitive areas.
B. It gives the respondent an opportunity to enlarge upon a topic which he may feel he has exhausted.

Probes can stiffen as well as reduce resistance; hence, they must be used with care. Also, there is always the possibility that the repondent may know little about a topic, or that he has forgotten his experiences in the topic area. Either way, injudicious probing may heighten his feeling that he should say something about the topic and thus lead to distortion (or even fabrication) on his part. If probing leads to problems, make a note of the area involved. Chances are the respondent will think about it; and it might prove to be fruitful to pursue it in a later interview. **Remember, overzealous probing in the face of resistance can seriously jeopardize the quality of the remaining material in the interview**. It is not worth the risk.

8. Are you permitting the respondent to "run" with a topic (within reason)? Remember the importance of memory association, especially with an older informant.

9. How are you seeking **clarification** of occasional answers? If you are often **interrupting**, this is generally poor technique (although sometimes, as during a "run," it is undeniably necessary). Normally it is best to return to the point after the respondent has finished.

10. If you find **notetaking** to be necessary, be alert to its effect on the continuity of the interview **and** on the attitude of the respondent. Proper names, foreign or unusual words or phrases, and the like often are crucial to the meaning or "sense" of entire blocks of information, and usually these should be written out. This is especially true when the interviewer is not likely to be the transcriber. In any event if you find that it was necessary to take many notes during the interview, allow enough time at the end to verify these with your respondent without rushing him or wearing our your welcome.

Robert E. Lowrie
American International College
Oral History Center

THE HOME FRONT DURING WORLD WAR II

In his course on World War II, Gene Rich of Springfield College invites older members of the community into his classroom to talk with students about their experiences on the "home front." He asks his volunteers to recall some of their feelings, attitudes, and beliefs, to suggest what their life was like, and to describe how it changed during the war years. Participants discuss the subject in a group, so that the ideas and memories of each individual may stimulate and validate those of the others.

To help his oral history subjects organize their thoughts and prepare for their visits, Rich gives them a list of topics, questions, and areas of interest in advance. Excerpts from this form are reproduced below:

Symbols of Sacrifice and Optimism:
e.g., "V" is for victory, Lucky Strike Green has gone to war, etc. How many can you remember? What did they mean to you?

Propaganda:
e.g., "loose lips sink ships" — posters, radio commentators, etc. How did the government, media, religious leaders, politicians promote the war effort? Did you ever question their reliability or purpose?

Social Problems:
How much were you aware of:
—the effects of moving to a new area or a new job?
—the increased divorce rate?
—the need for women to work?
—the absence of adults in the house from 8 AM to 6 PM?
—teenage gangs and the rise in juvenile delinquency?
—the increase in prostitution and "social diseases"?
—the problems of adjusting to a "young man-less" society?
—other problems?

VIOLENCE

Since 1974 John Bohstedt of Harvard University has taught a discussion course on collective violence in Britain, France, and America from 1750 to 1914.

Riots are a dramatic and revealing subject for study, since they precipitate for us otherwise obscure social relations among the crowd's members, their targets, and the authorities. My course begins with "pre-industrial" riots of the eighteenth century, riots which were a central form of community politics. We move on to ask under what circumstances riots became part of revolutionary crises in America (Massachusetts) and France, and how crowd violence helped bring constitutional change to England in 1832 and 1867. The General Strike of 1842 in England provides a rich case study of the interaction of Chartism, labor conflict, and police development. By the middle of the course, equipped with some substantive matter, we take up several more theoretical approaches to collective violence. We next move on to race riots in the American North, and then to slave resistance and the politics of racial dominance in the post-bellum South. Finally we talk about industrial violence in America in the 1870's and 1890's, and in Britain before the First World War.

On the one hand, riots throughout this period reflect most of the major social changes brought by the Industrial and Democratic Revolutions: the nationalization of the political horizons of the common people, class conflict, urbanization, police development, and ethnic conflicts entailed by the industrial recruitment of labor from peasant societies. But the story of collec-

tive violence also serves to challenge those theories of modernization that see crowd violence as an archaic feature of "pre-industrial" societies before the rise of labor movements. In fact, by trying to include a wide variety of riots, the course tries to go beyond the traditional outlines of labor history to a more inclusive concept of social conflict.

Discussions each week focus on a combination of broad overviews with one or two thoroughly analyzed case studies. The best case studies (like the best history) are those that relate a deep political, social, and economic context directly to the actors, forms, and consequences of crowd action. We also devote a second, one-hour discussion each week to specific eye-witness accounts of riots. Vital to the course are the students' case studies, which they bring in for class discussion. Within the limits of time and available resources, such case studies give students gratifying opportunities to use original source materials.

A vast amount of secondary literature is available, particularly for Europe before 1850, and for American violence throughout the period. Key course readings include Edward Thompson, "The Moral Economy of the English Crowd in the Eighteenth Century," *Past and Present* (February, 1971); George Rudé, *The Crowd in History* (1964); Pauline Maier, *From Resistance to Revolution* (1972); Robert Bezucha, *The Lyon Uprising of 1834* (1974); Charles Tilly, Louise Tilly, and Richard Tilly, *The Rebellious Century, 1830-1930* (1975); Eric Hobsbawn and George Rudé, *Captain Swing: A Social History of the Great Agricultural Uprising of 1830* (1968).

J.B.

AMERICAN REBELS

At the Dana Hall School in Wellesley, Massachusetts, John Means Spencer offers a semester course for juniors and seniors called "Violence in American History." A brief description follows:

The concept of covert and overt violence in American History is the theme of this course. One of the major objectives is to expose students to the plurality and multi-ethnic aspects of our culture.

In addition to films and filmstrips, students read Samuel Eliot Morison's *An Hour of American History* (1960) to gain background information and to learn how to gather data and develop their own hypotheses about our civilization.

The first unit focuses on what happened on Lexington Green, through investigation of contemporary sources and secondary works. Then students are asked to write their own textbook version of a similar event.

The second unit on the American Revolution allows students to simulate various roles. John Jakes's *The Rebels* (1975) gives students the opportunity to learn about the Revolution through the eyes of one family. Students write papers analyzing the question, "Are we going through a revolution in the 1960's and 1970's just as we did in the 1770's?"

Racism and pluralism are studied in the third unit. For context, students read Ernest Gaines's *The Autobiography of Miss Jane Pittman* (1971) and Otto Bettmann's *The Good Old Days — They Were Terrible* (1974).

J.M.S.

BLACKS IN BROCKTON

Willie A. Wilson, Jr., of Brockton High School (Massachusetts) has worked with students in his Afro-American History class to develop a slide-tape entitled "The Black Brocktonians."

My Afro-American History course began with a unit on Africa and then shifted to the United States for a look at slavery and the contributions of Blacks during the seventeenth and eighteenth centuries. We then spent one week on the history of Brockton, in order to develop a context for the slide-tape project. Each student was asked to write a character sketch of someone who lived in Brockton between 1744 and 1925, including an imaginative recreation of a "day-in-the-life" of that person. This assignment proved so successful that we spent an additional class period comparing the characters chosen and discussing the 1890's — the time period in which most of them lived.

This local history survey and multi-biographical study provided an excellent introduction to our project on Blacks in Brockton. To lead things off, I had the now elderly daughter of one of the early Black settlers visit the class. She reported personal reminiscences and also brought such historical materials as newspaper clippings and photographs. The excitement generated by her visit energized us for our first task: collecting as many prints and photographs as possible and making them into slides. Although some senior citizens were reluctant at first to lend us personal materials, word soon got around that we were "ok".

Our next project was oral history. Seeking to understand to what extent a sense of community existed among Blacks in Brock-

Members of the Messiah Baptist Church in the 1890's

ton between 1744 and 1925, students interviewed not only members of Black Brockton's most prominent families but also their own grandparents and even great-grandparents. Willa K. Baum's *Oral History for the Local Historical Society* (1969) proved to be an invaluable introduction to the techniques of oral history, both for myself and for the students.

The Black churches were, of course, an integral part of the Brockton Black community. And the pastors of these churches were extremely helpful in facilitating my students' research in their records.

As we began accumulating both slides and historical information, we started to shape our materials into the slide-tape

show. We wrote narration for the slides, created title slides to announce the sections of the presentation, and selected background music to reflect the historical periods represented.

Each year my Afro-American history class devotes part of its term to re-editing and improving the original presentation. I expect this process to continue as long as there is interest. The project has been a valuable learning experience. Students not only encounter a variety of disciplines (sociology, archaeology, etc.), but develop greater understanding of and respect for senior citizens.

W.A.W., Jr.

Church records provide valuable material for Black history. The first two Black churches in Brockton, the Lincoln Congregational Church and the Messiah Baptist Church, were both founded in 1897. That year, their members went on the first of several annual joint picnics. Trolleys were rented to take them to Mayflower Grove, a park in the neighboring town of Hanson.

CONFRONTING A BIASED AUTHOR

Rita E. Loos, who teaches at Framingham State College, recently asked students in her course on the history of American minorities to formulate their own critical evaluations of The Dispossessed Majority (*1973*) *by Wilmot Robertson. She discusses this experience below.*

I asked my students to evaluate one of four sections from this biased and distorted book. The students wrote reports examining first the background of the author, his education, area of expertise, etc. Then they considered the contents: What was the author's purpose in writing? What sources of information were cited? Were they valid?

Was the author biased or objective in his presentation?

As students read the sections chosen, they were amazed. They questioned the accuracy of many statements and openly wondered how such a work could be printed. A check of some footnotes indicated that the author had relied almost exclusively on secondary sources, some of questionable value, and that in many instances material was taken out of context.

Such an assignment helps students to develop critical thinking, acquaints them with the use of reference materials, exposes them to questions of style and proper research methods, and in the case of *The Dispossessed Majority* confronts them with an extreme viewpoint. Perhaps most important, they realize that books are not always true.

R.E.L.

Pearl Ashport Brooks, the first Black to graduate from Brockton High School (1907), lent the class many old photographs and daguerreotypes. This one shows her father, Lemuel Ashport, who was Brockton's first Black police officer. Born in Bridgewater, Lemuel served with the first Black regiment during the Civil War.

WOMEN'S HISTORY

Nancy F. Cott of Yale University teaches several courses on American social history. Her reading list for "American Women in the Nineteenth Century" follows.

AMERICAN WOMEN IN THE NINETEENTH CENTURY

I. THINKING ABOUT WOMEN'S HISTORY: A POTPOURRI

Ann Gordon, Mari Jo Buhle, and Nancy Schrom, **Women in American Society: An Historical Contribution** (Radical America Pamphlet, 1972), pp. 3-13, 21-24.

Aileen Kraditor, ed., **Up From the Pedestal** (1968), pp. 3-13, 21-24.

Nancy Chodorow, "Being and Doing," in Vivian Gornick and Barbara Moran, eds., **Women in Sexist Society** (1971).

Mirra Komarovsky, "Cultural Contradictions and Sex Roles," **American Journal of Sociology** (December, 1946).

Michele Wallace, "A Black Feminist's Search for Sisterhood," **Village Voice**, July 28, 1975, and Letters, August 4, 1975.

Helen Hacker, "Women as a Minority Group," **Social Forces** (October, 1950).

Kathleen Cleaver, "Interview," **Black Scholar** (December, 1971).

II. PRE-INDUSTRIAL BACKGROUND AND SOCIAL CHANGE

John Demos, **A Little Commonwealth: Family Life in Plymouth Colony** (1970), pp. 62-117.

Edmund Morgan, "The Puritans and Sex," **New England Quarterly** (December, 1942).

Gordon, Buhle, Schrom, "Women in American Society," pp. 17-38.

Nancy Cott, ed., **Root of Bitterness: Documents of the Social History of American Women** (1972), pp. 5-10, 59-90, 98-110.

Laila Hamamsy, "The Role of Women in Changing Navajo Society," **American Anthropologist** (February, 1957).

III. THE CULT OF DOMESTICITY

Gerda Lerner, "The Lady and the Mill-Girl: Changes in the Status of Women in the Age of Jackson," **Mid-continent American Studies Journal** (Spring, 1969).

Cott, **Root of Bitterness**, pp. 11-14, 113-125, 141-147, 157-177.

Daniel Scott Smith, "Family Limitation, Sexual Control, and Domestic Feminism in Victorian America," in Lois Banner and Mary Hartmann, eds., **Clio's Consciousness Raised** (1974).

Carroll Smith-Rosenberg, "The Hysterical Woman: Sex Roles and Role Conflict in 19th Century America," **Social Research** (Winter, 1972)

William R. Taylor, **Cavalier and Yankee: The Old South and American National Character** (1961), pp. 115-122.

IV. NORTHERN WOMEN: VARIETIES OF EXPERIENCE

Cott, **Root of Bitterness**, pp. 126-140, 148-156, 223-255.

Edith Abbott, **Women in Industry** (1909), chapters 3-5.

Norman Ware, **The Industrial Worker, 1840-1860** (1924), pp. 48-55; chapters 5, 7, 9.

Mary Wilkins Freeman, "The Revolt of 'Mother'," in Lee R. Edwards and Arlyn Diamond, eds., **American Voices, American Women** (1973).

Christine Stansell and Johnny Faragher, "Women and their Families on the Oregon Trail, 1842-1867," **Feminist Studies** (Spring, 1975).

V. THE SOUTHERN LADY

Anne F. Scott, **The Southern Lady: From Pedestal to Politics** (1970), chapters 1-4.

Edmund Wilson, **Patriotic Gore** (1962), pp. 258-298.

Taylor, **Cavalier and Yankee**, pp. 162-176.

VI. WOMEN IN BONDAGE

Gerda Lerner, ed., **Black Women in White America** (1972), pp. 1-72.

Eugene Genovese, **Roll, Jordan, Roll** (1974), pp. 327-365, 450-475, 494-501, 524-535.

Angela Davis, "The Black Woman's Role in the Community of Slaves," **Black Scholar** (December, 1971).

VII. WOMEN'S BODIES

Cott, **Root of Bitterness**, pp. 18-21, 263-308.

Lerner, **Black Women**, pp. 155-159, 172-188.

Charles E. Rosenberg, "Sexuality, Class and Role in 19th-Century America," **American Quarterly** (May, 1973).

Nancy Cott, "Passionlessness; An Interpretation" (xeroxed manuscript).

Carl N. Degler, "What Ought to Be and What Was: Women's Sexuality in the Nineteenth Century," **American Historical Review** (December, 1974).

Linda Gordon, "Voluntary Motherhood: The Beginnings of Feminist Birth Control Ideas in the U.S.," in Banner and Hartmann, eds., **Clio's Consciousness Raised.**

VIII. WOMEN'S MINDS

Barbara Welter, "The Feminization of American Religion, 1800-1860," in Banner and Hartmann, eds., **Clio's Consciousness Raised.**

Caroll Smith-Rosenberg, "Beauty, the Beast, and the Militant Woman: A Case Study in Sex Roles and Social Stress in Jacksonian America," **American Quarterly** (October, 1971).

Keith Melder, "Ladies Bountiful: Organized Women's Benevolence in 19th-Century America," **American Quarterly** (October, 1971).

Horace Adams, "A Puritan Wife on the Frontier," **Mississippi Valley Historical Review** (June, 1940).

Lerner, **Black Women**, pp. 75-107, 561-574.

Alice Rossi, ed., **The Feminist Papers** (1974), pp. 144-158.

Elizabeth Stuart Phelps, "The Story of Avis," in Edwards and Diamond, **American Voices, American Women.**

IX. FEMINISM, I

Kraditor, **Up From the Pedestal**, pp. 13-21, 45-66, 71-73, 148-150, 220-230.

Rossi, **The Feminist Papers**, pp. 241-322, 378-396, 413-430.

X. FEMINISM, II

Ellen DuBois, "The 19th Century Woman Suffrage Movement: Suffrage as a Total Ideology," **Feminist Studies** (Fall, 1975).

James McPherson, "Abolitionists, Woman Suffrage, and the Negro, 1865-1869," **Mid-America** (January, 1965).

Kraditor, **Up From the Pedestal**, pp. 189-219, 243-287.

Rossi, **The Feminist Papers**, pp. 566-598.

XI. PATTERNS OF WOMEN'S EMPLOYMENT

Robert Smuts, **Women and Work in America** (1959), pp. 6-24, 38-58, 69-98, 106-109.

Cott, **Root of Bitterness**, pp. 21-24, 311-347.

Rosalyn Baxandall, Linda Gordon, and Susan Reverby, eds., **America's Working Women** (1976), pp. 85-131.

Lerner, **Black Women**, pp. 226-231.

James Kenneally, "Women and the Trade Unions, 1870-1920," **Labor History** (Winter, 1973).

XII. THE "NEW WOMAN'S" WORK

Smuts, **Women and Work**, pp. 110-142.

Ellen Keniston and Kenneth Keniston, "An American Anachronism: The Image of Women and Work," **American Scholar** (Summer, 1963-1964).

William O'Neill, **Everyone was Brave: A History of Feminism in America** (1971), pp. 84-102.

Cott, **Root of Bitterness**, pp. 351-362.

Rossi, **The Feminist Papers**, pp. 599-612.

Jill Conway, "Woman Reformers and American Culture, 1870-1930," **Journal of Social History** (Winter, 1971-1972).

Lerner, **Black Women**, pp. 333-337.

Nancy Schrom Dye, "Creating a Feminist Alliance: Sisterhood and Class Conflict in the N.Y. Women's Trade Union League, 1903-1914," **Feminist Studies** (Fall, 1975).

The Common Women Collective has published a comprehensive annotated bibliography, **Women in U.S. History** (1976). It is available for $2.00 plus 25 cents postage at 5 Upland Road, Cambridge, Massachusetts 02140.

Clearinghouse

Established in 1970, the Clearinghouse on Women's Studies collects information about courses and programs offered at colleges and high schools across the country, contributed by more than 6,000 teachers. To share its findings, the Clearinghouse issues a series of publications, including the **Women's Studies Newsletter**, which provides bibliographies along with project and course descriptions. The Clearinghouse also serves as a resource center for teachers, curriculum developers, and program planners. Address: P.O. Box 334, Old Westbury, New York 11568.

THE NEW GOVERNESS

— **Peterson's Magazine** (January, 1872)

WOMEN IN REVOLUTIONARY CHINA

One way history teachers can introduce students to the experiences of unfamiliar groups is through role-playing. Eugene Lubot, formerly of Wheaton College, has designed the following exercise for use in teaching modern Chinese history. For a fuller discussion of role-playing in history teaching, see "Personality in History."

I. Setting

The setting is a village in China in 1949. It has recently been liberated by the Chinese Communists and the women are trying to *fan-shen* (that is, "turn over" or overthrow all the old values). The women of the village have been organized into a Women's Association, but the Chinese Communists have left the village for more urgent business elsewhere. To test the level of consciousness of the villagers, the Communists have asked the village to draft a Declaration of Women's rights. The Communists hope the Declaration can obtain the approval of the three major groups in the village: the Women's Association, the Husbands, and the Mothers-in-law. If this is impossible, the Communists have left instructions that a Declaration be drafted which has the approval of two groups out of the three.

II. Procedures

You will be divided into three role-playing groups:
1. Women of the Women's Association
2. Husbands
3. Mothers-in-law

The objective will be to draft a Declaration of Women's Rights which is acceptable to all three groups. Members of a group may disagree with each other in the process of discussion, but a majority vote will determine the group position on any specific issue. If it proves impossible, as well it might, to draft a Declaration acceptable to all three groups, then participants should turn their attention to the business of bargains, compromises, and trade-offs in an attempt to form an alliance between two groups which can agree upon a Declaration. Whichever group is left out will obviously be faced with a Declaration unfavorable to its interests, so it should frantically try to detach one of the members of the alliance by offering it a better deal. The simulation will end when a Declaration is drafted and signed by the leaders of at least two of the groups.

III. Issues

At a minimum, the Declaration of Women's Rights shall address the following issues:

a. Whether women and men should enjoy equal rights under the law.

b. Whether women should have the right to move about freely and to organize themselves into a Women's Association.

c. Whether women and men should have the right to choose their own marriage partners; and whether each should have the same rights with regard to divorce.

d. Whether women should be allowed to accept paid employment, and whether women and men should receive equal pay for equal work.

E.L.

WOMEN AND THE ECONOMY

Susan Naigles of Hamilton-Wenham Regional High School (Massachusetts) has developed an approach for studying how the economic role of women changed as the American economic system changed from

The sewing room at A.T. Stewart's Retail Store, New York City, *from* Frank Leslie's Illustrated Newspaper *(April 4, 1875)*

agriculture to industry. Students ask the following questions of different women in different historical periods:

1. What goods did they produce and use?
2. What services did they provide and use?
3. What resources (human, natural, capital) did they use to produce goods or provide services?
4. What machines (technology) did they use to produce these goods or provide these services?
5. What part did they play in distributing these goods and services?

To analyze the economic role of women in the twentieth-century industrial economy, the class is divided into groups of five or six. Each group selects a woman from the community to interview — a lawyer, housewife, waitress, factory worker, etc. From each interview, which relies on the economic role questions above, a slide-tape is produced, which then becomes a resource for another exercise. Each student assumes a twentieth-century female occupational role and writes a five-page analysis comparing and contrasting that role with the role of an early nineteenth-century farmwife. By so doing, it is possible to analyze production, consumption, distribution, technology, and resources, while also imagining the feelings of a farmwife performing her economic tasks.

Naigles developed this curriculum model in association with the Three Dimensional Project at Old Sturbridge Village. A more detailed description is available, along with models by teachers on other subjects, each for $1. For copies, or further information about the Project, write the Museum Education Department, Old Sturbridge Village, Sturbridge, Massachusetts 01566.

FAMILY HISTORY

Kathleen D. Lyman and Richard B. Lyman, Jr., of Simmons College, summarize below their experience assigning family history papers.

We ask students in our course on the history of the family to write histories of their own families. We emphasize that they should organize their papers around specific themes or questions. We have been very clear that we do not want just a padded genealogy or a vaguely descriptive narrative.

This task may present difficulties, since some students experience problems of distance: either too much physical distance to do an effective job in the course of a semester or too little emotional distance to poke around in topics that are possibly very sensitive or controversial.

A family history is much harder to evaluate than the standard high school or college term paper. So much of the student's own self is involved, and we have to be careful not to appear to be evaluating the quality of the student's family life or background. We instead look at the paper's research methodology, the types of questions posed, the clarity of presentation, the use of source materials available, the use of interviews with family members, and whether the student places his or her family's history into a broader historical setting. Judged by these standards, the papers seemed to be about twice as good and as thoroughly researched as any we have had in courses of a comparable level.

K.D.L.
R.B.L., Jr.

ANONYMOUS FAMILIES HISTORY PROJECT

More than 400 teachers have participated in the Anonymous Families History Project, a network of students and instructors interested in family history. They use a brief guide, "Writing the Social History of One's Family . . .," written by Richard D. Brown of the University of Connecticut and Tamara K. Hareven of Clark University, with the assistance of Ronald J. Grele of the Ford Foundation's Oral History Project. The guide explains how to conduct an oral history interview, lists both primary and secondary sources on family history, and describes how students may deposit their completed family histories in the archives of the Anonymous Families History Project at the Social Welfare Archives of the University of Minnesota, Minneapolis, Minnesota 55455. Reproduced below is a list of questions from the guide that students might use when interviewing family members. For a copy of the complete guide or for more information, contact Tamara K. Hareven, Department of History, Clark University, Worcester, Massachusetts 01610.

QUESTIONS FOR INTERVIEWS OF RELATIVES

The Internal Experience of the Family

I. Dwelling and organization of family life:

1. Did family members other than the parents and their children live in the same apartment or house, in the same building, along the same street, or in the same neighborhood?

2. Did married daughters or sons continue to live in their parents' household? Did aging parents live in their children's households, in their own dwellings, in retirement communities, or in old age homes?

3. How did the family organize its living space? Who slept in what room? How was the work and living space divided? How crowded was the household?

4. Were there servants and boarders living with the family?

II. Social organizations and family activities:

1. What were the daily schedules of family members? How did they spend their time at home and their holidays?

2. Who visited whom, how frequently and over what periods of time?

3. What kind of family celebrations were held? Were there family reunions held? How were weddings, baptisms, funerals and other ceremonies held? Who attended? Where were they held?

III. Decision making and status in the family:

1. How were key decisions made on moving, schooling, occupational choice, and approval of marriage?

2. How were decisions on daily family business made (budget, housekeeping, etc.)?

3. Who disciplined the children and by what means?

4. Aside from parents, what other adults participated in disciplining the children? Did grandparents participate in rearing their grandchildren?

5. What types of conflict occurred in the family and what were the responses?

6. Were there persons treated as "Black Sheep"? How did this affect their relationship to family members?
7. How were family members ranked (sex, age, ability, occupation, success) in terms of their privileges and obligations?
8. What were the sitting arrangements during meals?

IV. Aid and responsibility:

1. Did parents help their children in college, or business? Did mature sons and daughters support their aging parents?
2. Who cared for sick or dependent family members?
3. How did well-to-do members of the family relate to those of lesser means?

V. Family and property:

1. Who owned property in the family and how did they manage it?
2. Did the women receive dowries?
3. Who inherited what?

VI. Careers and opportunity:

1. At what age did sons and daughters leave home to embark on their careers? Did women leave earlier than men?
2. Did sons follow their fathers' occupations?
3. What was the family's attitude towards the work of women?
4. What influence did parents and grandparents have on the occupational choices of their grandchildren?
5. What criteria and priorities did family members set for "success" (financial, occupational, residential, scholarly, "good marriages")?

VII. Questions pertaining to the life cycle:

1. How were babies treated in the family?
2. Up to what age was a child considered a "child"?
3. Was "adolescence" recognized as a special stage?
4. At what age was a young person expected to take on adult responsibilities?
5. What were attitudes towards aging?
6. Did aging parents continue to live with their children?

VIII. Migration and the family:

1. Who in the family was the first to emigrate to the United States or to move from one location to another?
2. What relatives followed?
3. Why did family members decide to migrate and relocate?
4. What contact continued with the old country?
5. How often did family members return to areas they had moved from?
6. Did they remember their places of origin with nostalgia?

Factors External to the Family

When interviewing members of the family, one should inquire about historical events that may have had an impact on the history of the family. Examples of such events or developments may include:

Wars, depressions, periods of prosperity, emancipation of slaves, Jim Crow laws, immigration policies, military service, employment patterns, welfare services, urban renewal, technological change, transportation, and mass media.

R.D.B.
T.K.H.

BASEBALL FROM THE BOTTOM UP

According to Ronald Story of Clark University, the history of baseball is a subject that may usefully focus an inquiry into the experience of the American common people.

Baseball was one of the earliest mass entertainment industries. The movement of this sport from infancy to maturity reflects the emergence of an urban mass with leisure time and disposable income; and the simultaneous efforts of entertainment entrepreneurs — in theater, cinema, cabarets, publishing, and recording as well as sports — to attract, control, shape, and exploit it for commercial purposes. I use slides of baseball players, fans, and ballparks to illustrate these developments. The first slides cover the period 1860-1890, when the players were rough and ill-paid professionals, but the parks remained comparatively rustic and the au-

diences comparatively small, decorous, and genteel, as they had been in amateur days. The second group of slides covers the period 1890-1910, when the status and image of the players became more respectable, the parks were more urban in setting, and the audiences increasingly large, working-class, and unruly. The last slides deal with the years 1910-1925, when the parks were modernized and enlarged and the crowds became more restrained in behavior and more homogeneously middle-class in appearance.

I have also made baseball the focus of an investigative methods course, which originally developed as a "workshop" at the University of Massachusetts, Amherst. This is intended to introduce students to techniques of historical inquiry. Centering on the famous Black Sox pay-off scandal, I draw on recorded interviews with retired

ballplayers and transparencies of Chicago transportation and neighborhood developments, along with slides of ball parks, crowds, and players.

R.S.

Hilltop Park, New York. c. 1905

Baseball grounds, Chicago, 1883

Fidel at bat

Quantifying the Past

introduction

Although innovative teaching strategies in New England have often reflected and sometimes even anticipated the latest scholarly trends, quantification in the classroom has lagged well behind quantification in historical scholarship. Quantitative methodology has been a powerful tool in the writing of social, political, economic, and intellectual history, but only occasionally in history teaching.

Yet the statistical concepts and techniques used by quantitative historians are not mystical; they are readily accessible to both teachers and students without special training. "Many high school students of average mathematics ability," notes Mitchell P. Lichtenberg, Social Studies Director of the Franklin (Massachusetts) schools, "can easily grasp rudimentary statistical concepts. After all, counting, averaging, ranking, sampling, and measures of simple correlation require little more than the accurate application of basic arithmetical skills." Even the most humanistically trained historian can understand and do some simple counting.

Increasingly, New England history teachers have demonstrated that quantification can be integrated into the classroom. They have found that tax lists, voting returns, and land deeds can interest and inform history students.

Gathering and analyzing quantitative data may help to engage students more directly in the process of historical inquiry. Through such work they become more acutely aware of the possibilities and limitations of historical method.

Even more importantly, quantitative history can sensitize students to the experience of millions of ordinary people often ignored by standard historical accounts. The Irish laborer of Newburyport, the Swedish domestic of Worcester, and the displaced artisan of Amiens become real and significant historical actors, often for the first time, to students who work with nineteenth-century census manuscripts. Thus "quantitative history," in the words of M.I.T. historian Bruce Mazlish, "is not merely the demanding use of computer skills . . . . It is an attempt also at a reorientation and redefinition of history itself."

"Tonight, we're going to let the statistics speak for themselves."

Drawing by Koren; © 1974
The New Yorker Magazine, Inc.

QUANTITATIVE HISTORY: Prospects and Problems

Robert W. Fogel of Harvard University, co-author of the controversial quantitative study of nineteenth-century slavery Time on the Cross *(1974), presents below a brief report on the latest trends and techniques in the field. Following, G. B. Warden of the Cambridge Historical Society offers some cautionary notes.*

THE STATUS OF QUANTITATIVE HISTORY

What is the status of the effort to apply quantitative methods to history? The movement for the systematic application of behavioral models and various related mathematical and statistical methods to historical analysis is about two decades old. This type of work now has a firm foothold in the historical profession.

The mathematical approach has developed most rapidly within the field of economic history. The new economic history, also called cliometrics and econometric history, has become the predominant form of research in this field, at least in the United States. The majority of the articles published in the main economic history journals of the United States are now quite mathematical, and cliometricians predominate in the leadership of the Economic History Association.

The progress of the mathematical approach in the mainstream of history, while less rapid, has nevertheless been substantial. Political, social, and even intellectual history have all had their quantifiers. There are research groups engaged in the application of mathematical methods to history in at least a dozen American universities. Several national committees have come into being to encourage the application of mathematical methods to history. In 1965 the Mathematical Social Science Board (MSSB) established a History Advisory Committee through which it has organized conferences and advanced research institutes on various subjects which represent the frontier of research by quantitative historians. In conjunction with Princeton University Press, MSSB is sponsoring a ten-volume series entitled Studies in Quantitative History.

The American Historical Association has an *ad hoc* Committee on Quantitative Data in History that is concerned with the collection of quantitative information and its transcription into machine-readable form. The Inter-University Consortium for Political Research (ICPR) has established a Historical Data Archives that is collecting and putting into machine-readable form large quantities of political, economic, and social information for both the United States and France. ICPR also runs an annual summer training institute on mathematical methods for historians. The first meeting of the newly formed Social Science History Association took place in 1976. Three journals have been established to promote quantitative history — the *Historical Methods Newsletter*, the *Journal of Interdisciplinary History*, and *Social Science History*.

To what kinds of issues should quantitative methods be applied? Formal quantitative methods have their most obvious application in the analysis of the behavior of groups. Indeed, without the aid of formal statistical methods it is not possible to describe adequately the characteristics — let alone to explain their evolution over time — of such large groups as socio-economic classes (workers, capitalists, peasants, slaves), populations of national or subnational political units (provinces, states, cities), political and social elites (legislators, revolutionary leaders, bishops, nobles), or other specific social, economic, or political categories (immigrants, members of religious orders, dissenters, taxpayers, voters).

Quantitative methods are essential if historians are to succeed in shifting the attention of their discipline from a preoccupation with exceptional individuals to concentration on the life and times of common people. Indeed, the application of quantitative methods in history has opened up the possiblity that with respect to such issues as the evolution of the family, the determinants of occupational mobility, and the effect of religion on political and social behavior we may soon be able to say more about the experiences of ordinary people than of exceptional individuals.

R.W.F.

Adapted from the **American Historical Review** (April, 1975).

PITFALLS OF QUANTITATIVE HISTORY

Valuable as quantification is for understanding demographic trends, census figures, price series, content analysis, voting records, and measures of inequality in the past, there are some pitfalls which history teachers need to know lest they get carried away with the illusions of certainty.

For example, in his recent television survey Alistair Cooke repeated John Adams's famous statement that one third of Americans were for the American Revolution, one third against it, and one third indifferent. Like many others, Cooke failed to notice that Adams was talking about American reactions to the *French* revolution. That blooper we may call an error of context.

Why did so many of the Founding Fathers — except the Adamses — have no surviving, legitimate male children to carry on the family name and create an American aristocracy? Franklin, Jefferson, Hamilton, Madison, and Washington had no children, no sons, only daughters, or no legitimate sons. One can create an iron-clad but totally erroneous statistical argument that a 100% negative correlation existed between having sons and a family name ending in "n". That we may call an error of coincidental inference.

Looking for the effects of World War II on the population, researchers noted that the Census of 1950 showed an astronomically large increase in the number of fourteen-year-old widowers, an invasion of New England by young Indian males, and other inexplicable anomalies. A check revealed that in about 8% of the millions of punch cards the columns for age, sex, marital status, family position, etc., had been erroneously shifted one column to the right. That is an error of method.

Two studies of family size on the same South Pacific island appeared at the same time by reputable scholars but with widely different totals. Why? One researcher began with a definition based on bloodlines; the other based his findings on observation

of people in the household. That is an error of definition.

The list of statistical "horror stories" could be endless. To avoid perpetrating your own, a few caveats need to be kept in mind.

First, numbers are best thought of as adjectives, not as nouns; if you think of numbers as having some independent substantial existence, you are in trouble.

Second, numbers need to be translated into prose whenever they appear; like any "facts," numbers do not speak for themselves and need to be communicated in human terms.

Third, numbers in history suffer from the misleading impression that they provide a scientific, mathematically precise, and intellectually coherent image of reality; that misconception has led to so many errors that scientists prefer instead to see percentages, averages, and the like as measures of *probability*, not absolute certainty.

Fourth, numbers are good for answering number-questions (how much? how often? within what range? etc.). Most errors in the method and inferences of quantification arise because people try to use numbers to answer non-number questions (why? why not? how?).

Finally and most important, except for tracing, say, price series or aggregates of things, numbers have a lamentable tendency to degrade human beings by reducing the complications of human experience into lifeless averages while tending to exclude the infinite exceptions which make living messy and interesting. The telephone company and the IRS provide telling examples of this tendency.

G.B.W.

Quantitative History Reading List

Traditionally trained historians may be unfamiliar with the techniques and technologies of quantitative history, and thus reluctant to introduce them into their classrooms. In fact, much quantitative history is not mathematically sophisticated; a working competence can be acquired by reading a few basic works.

Some guides to doing quantitative history include: Edward Shorter, **The Historian and the Computer** (1975); Charles M. Dollar and Richard Jensen, **Historians' Guide to Statistics** (1975); and Roderick Floud, **Quantitative Methods for Historians** (1974). Hubert Blalock, **Social Statistics** (1972), is a standard statistical text, useful for historians. The Statistical Package for the Social Sciences (SPSS) is a computer package readily adapted for historical work and available in most university computers.

For an introduction to the large and growing literature of quantitative history, consult: Robert P. Swierenga, "Computers and American History: The Impact of the 'New' Generation," **Journal of American History** (March, 1974); Richard Jensen, "Quantitative American Studies: The State of the Art," **American Quarterly** (Fall, 1974); Val R. Lorwin and Jacob M. Price, eds., **The Dimensions of the Past: Materials, Problems, and Opportunities for Quantitative Work in History** (1972).

The following articles deal specifically with the uses of quantitative history in teaching: Charles Stephenson, "Approaches to Social Science History: Quantification in the Classroom," **Teaching History** (Fall, 1976); Michael P. Weber, "Quantification and the Teaching of American Urban History," **History Teacher** (May, 1975); and Donald DeBats and Paul Bourke, "The United States Manuscript Census as a Teaching Aid," **Historical Methods Newsletter** (March, 1974).

TEACHING WHAT COUNTS IN HISTORY

At Northeastern University, Ballard C. Campbell offers a course on "Social Science Methodology for Historians."

My course acquaints undergraduates of any major with the logic and techniques of social scientific history. It is designed for 25 class meetings. Part I introduces the premises of social scientific inquiry and discusses its relation to historical analysis. Emphasis is placed on concept formation and the relation between description and explanation as interacting components of social scientific research. Part II surveys techniques of quantitative analysis, with the goal of demonstrating how language and ideas can be translated into measurable entities. Emphasis centers on the function of data manipulation rather than on applied statistics. No mathematical or statistical background is assumed. Particular attention is given to index construction as the basic descriptive tool of quantitative analysis and to the objectives of statistical association. Part III uses a case study approach to illustrate modes of interdisciplinary history.

I. Foundations of Social Scientific Inquiry
  1. History and the social sciences
  2. Concepts, models, hypotheses, theory
  3. Research design
  4. Description and explanation

II. Basic Quantitative Techniques
  1. Data
  2. Index construction
  3. Descriptive statistics
  4. Statistics of association: crosstabulation
  5. Statistics of association: correlation

III. Case Studies in Interdisciplinary History
  1. Population and family
  2. Social structure
  3. Social mobility
  4. Public opinion

5. Political behavior
6. Economic history

Students are assigned two quantitative exercises that complement class presentation of fundamentals of data analysis. Experience has shown that applied problems are essential for students to understand fully the mechanics of certain statistical procedures. The data consist of the percentage of the Democratic Presidential vote in 1960 and 1972, median family income, metropolitanism, and the sectional identification of the American states. Computations for 50 states are easily managed by hand, but punched cards are available for students who wish to use the computer.

The substantive focus of the exercises is on the sources of McGovern's strengths and weaknesses in the 1972 Presidential election. Crosstabulations between the McGovern vote and the variables income, metropolitanism, and section, for example, indicate that McGovern did best in states with higher median income and large metropolitan areas and in the northeast and midwest. By controlling the variable section, however, students can see that the income correlation was partially the result of McGovern's poor showing in the south, where income was comparatively low. Analysis of the change in the Democratic vote between 1960 and 1972 illustrates that section (namely, the south) explained a greater proportion of McGovern's losses relative to Kennedy's strength than did income and metropolitanism. The assignment also requires students to summarize their findings concisely in non-technical prose. The exercise can generate added interest by allowing students to suggest explanations for the variations in McGovern's vote.

B.C.C.

State	McGovern 1972 (%)	Kennedy 1960 (%)	Median Family Income 1969 [1] ($) in 100's	Metropolitan 1970 [2] (%)
Alabama	25.5	56.8	73	52
Alaska	34.6	49.1	124	0*
Arizona	30.4	44.4	92	74
Arkansas	30.7	50.2	63	31
California	41.5	49.6	107	93
Colorado	34.6	44.9	95	72
Conn.	40.1	53.7	118	83
Delaware	39.2	50.6	102	70
Florida	27.8	48.5	83	69
Georgia	24.7	62.6	82	50
Hawaii	37.5	50.0*	115	82
Idaho	26.1	46.2	84	16
Illinois	40.5	50.0*	110	80
Indiana	33.3	44.6	100	62
Iowa	40.5	43.2	90	36
Kansas	29.5	39.1	87	42
Kentucky	34.8	46.4	74	40
Louisiana	28.3	50.4	75	55
Maine	38.5	43.0	82	21
Maryland	37.4	53.6	111	84
Mass.	54.2	60.2	108	85
Michigan	41.8	50.9	110	78
Minn.	46.1	50.6	99	57
Miss.	19.6	36.3	61	18
Mo.	37.7	50.3	89	64
Mont.	37.9	48.6	85	24
Neb.	29.5	37.9	86	43
Nev.	36.3	51.2	107	81
New Hamp.	34.9	46.6	97	27
New Jersey	36.8	50.0*	114	80
New Mex.	36.6	50.2	78	31
New York	41.2	52.5	106	86
North Car.	28.9	52.1	78	37
North Dak.	35.8	44.5	78	12
Ohio	38.1	46.7	103	78
Oklahoma	24.0	41.0	77	50
Oregon	42.3	47.4	95	61
Penn.	39.1	51.1	96	79
Rhode Is.	46.8	63.6	97	85
South Car.	27.7	51.2	76	39
South Dak.	45.5	41.8	75	14
Tenn.	29.7	45.8	74	49
Texas	33.3	50.5	85	73
Utah	26.4	45.2	93	78
Vermont	36.5	41.4	89	0*
Virginia	30.1	47.0	90	61
Wash.	38.6	48.3	104	66
W. Virginia	36.4	52.7	74	31
Wis.	43.7	48.0	101	58
Wyoming	30.5	45.0	89	0*

1. Median money income of families. Based on sample.
2. Metropolitan: population (% of total) residing in standard metropolitan statistical area (SMSA).

*Not applicable (no data); no population residing in SMSA.

Source: U.S. Bureau of the Census, STATISTICAL ABSTRACT OF THE UNITED STATES: 1974.

TEACHING QUANTITATIVE
HISTORY IN THE HIGH SCHOOL

Paul J. Keaney of the Brooks School in North Andover, Massachusetts, introduces 11th and 12th graders to the uses of mathematics in historical analysis.

"Quantitative History" was a one-term course with second-year algebra as a prerequisite. Two of the nine weeks were devoted to an independent research project; the other seven involved study of selected topics in various historical subjects requiring mathematics.

One topic focused on the membership and voting records of Congressmen. Allan G. Bogue, *et al.*, "Members of the House of Representatives and the Processes of Modernization, 1789-1960," *Journal of American History* (September, 1976), showed how to tabulate the characteristics of individuals and groups as a way of understanding their behavior in the legislative process. Jerome M. Clubb and Santa Traugott, "Partisan Cleavage and Cohesion in the House of Representatives, 1861-1974," *Journal of Interdisciplinary History* (Winter, 1977), led the students into more advanced mathematics, such as correlation coefficients, to understand party alignments and roll-call analysis.

In a second topic students reviewed standard interpretations of the causes of the Civil War and compared them with the model constructed by Gerald Gunderson in "The Origin of the American Civil War," *Journal of Economic History* (December, 1974). In analyzing trends in population, regional change, agricultural wealth, industrialization, and urban growth, students were introduced to sophisticated measures of inequalities and changes over time, so

that they could understand the series of events leading to secession and violence.

The study of legislative behavior in general and the more particular issues of the Civil War provided background for the research project, in which the students developed computer programs for analyzing the content of speeches and arguments by leading statesmen in the years leading up to the Civil War.

P.J.K.

TEACHING HISTORY TO TECHNICAL STUDENTS

Larry Bucciarelli, an engineer himself, teaches history to technical students at M.I.T. For a description of his course, see page 76.

The actual engineering of technology provides rich associations to the past for technical students, and we nurture their inclination to inquire into mechanical workings. They can often understand historical developments by replicating the calculations and decisions of individuals in the past. In teaching about the establishment of the Lowell textile mills, we show students a picture of the Merrimack River. After giving them the flow of the water, seasonal variations included, and the available head, we ask them to estimate the amount of power ideally available. They then judge how many looms and spindles could be driven. They compute this calculation in much the same way as it was done by the mechanics and entrepreneurs who viewed the rapids for the first time in 1820. Dependence on water power to run the mills made the control of the water rights of the Merrimack crucial to the mill owners. By understanding the technical issue involved, students are led into a discussion of the broader political

and economic implications of technological enterprise. This is also an opportunity for us to discuss how human technological activity moves to smooth out and control the irregularities of nature — human nature as well as the nature outside of us.

L.B.

1. In Lowell "1 Mill Power" entitled a mill owner to draw 25 cubic feet of water per second at a head of 30 feet.
2. 1 Mill Power after losses was found to be sufficient to power all machinery in a mill containing approximately 4,000 spindles. (Losses consumed 33% of that 1 Mill Power.) The Merrimack Mill, the first built in Lowell, had 35,704 spindles. How many Mill Powers were required to power the Merrimack?
3. Using the data below describing average daily flows for the twelve months of the year, and assuming a fall of 30 feet, calculate the Mill Powers **theoretically** available during the month with the highest flow rate and during the month with the lowest flow rate.
4. What do you suppose were the economic and legal implications of the discrepancy between the month with the highest flow rate and the month with the lowest?

Rank Order of Monthly Flows each Year	Average Daily flow of Ranked Months in Cubic Feet of Water per Second
1st (highest)	21,274
2nd	13,462
3rd	10,078
4th	8,315
5th	7,264
6th	5,736
7th	4,632
8th	3,707
9th	3,072
10th	2,439
11th	1,999
12th (lowest)	1,655

COMPARATIVE CITIES: A Computer Teaching File

R. Burr Litchfield and Howard Chuda-coff of Brown University teach both quantitative techniques and comparative social history with computer data concerning four mid-nineteenth-century cities. Below, Litchfield explains their approach.

A few years ago, at Brown, my colleague Howard Chudacoff and I were considering the problems of introducing undergraduates and beginning graduate students to the comparative study of social, urban, demographic, and family history. We concluded that to a large degree we were teaching a kind of literary criticism. That is, we were taking Thesis A from some source in the secondary literature and having students re-word it into Thesis B; a third element, evidence that might support or disprove the initial statement, was unavailable, difficult to use in the classroom, or of a nature such that its use involved technical problems and costs insurmountable for students in the brief time allowed.

This was an awkward situation, especially since we ourselves, in our separate research activities, were engaged in analyzing large computer files of data designed to discover something of the lives of large groups of people in the social and urban world of the past. For these there are few diaries, letters, or eye-witness reports, and such that have remained require understanding in the context of the evidence of censuses, tax lists, and vital records. Materials of particular importance for the historical investigation of common people are the manuscript schedules of the nineteenth-century census, and we noticed that history students without knowledge of statistics, or the nature of these and similar sources, have difficulty comprehending the new fields of investigation that have developed in this area.

AMIENS

Thus we set out to design parallel undergraduate courses in European and American history that would permit students to gain experience by testing new hypotheses with real data. We received initial funding from the National Endowment for the Humanities, obtained microfilms of censuses, and began work in 1972. Initially, in "Comparative Cities," we worked as we would have in the past, asking each of the 20 students enrolled to code 100 individuals from the census, and thus acquired an initial sample of 2,000 for class use. Careful attention was given to designing a method for coding in the maximum of detail, so that the data

could later be used in the most flexible manner possible. Unfortunately, although students learned a good deal about coding, by the end of the term they were too worn out to devote much energy to analysis of the problems with which we had begun. So the following summer we hired four coders to code 40,000 records. This data was edited, elaborated, and programmed through SPSS (Statistical Package for the Social Sciences), a well developed, widely available, and easy-to-use statistical package. The next fall we started out with a large computer file, and were thus able to begin the course at a more satisfactory analytical level.

We wanted to organize materials that would illustrate a large theme of interest to students from a variety of different points of view, and that could be used for instruction at other institutions than Brown. A central theme of developing interest in social history, for which the manuscript censuses provide basic information, has been the tension between industrialization and modernization of the nineteenth-century city. But a problem with all studies in this area is the narrow band of time for which workable censuses exist, in both Europe and America. So as to enlarge the scope of study, we decided to proceed with comparisons in space rather than in time, and thus chose four cities at different stages of industrialization and of the demographic transition.

These were Pisa in 1841, a traditional Italian city that still showed the pattern of pre-industrial Europe; Amiens in 1851, an old administrative and artisanal textile center in northern France undergoing the effects of commercial expansion; Stockport in 1841 and 1851, a "classic" cotton factory town of the English industrial revolution;

and Providence, R.I., in 1865, a city along the American East Coast experiencing both industrial transformation and a large influx of European migrants.

The approach of the course has been from hypothesis to evidence. The first three weeks are devoted to discussion of social history. Then there is a short period in which students are introduced to SPSS and the census file. The point of the course is historical problem solving rather than computer technology, so we have tried to keep computer techniques in the background and to introduce statistical concepts gradually, as the need arises from the problems to be solved.

For the next three weeks students prepare reports on specific topics. At the end of the term they submit final papers that have often grown out of these reports. These final papers may focus on technical problems of demographic or family history based on the application of statistical analysis to the basic data, or they may be more speculative — as when students identify an occupational or ethnic group and seek out literature and other sources to flesh out and explain more fully the life-patterns observed.

Because of the cost of computer time, we have had to cut down the size of the samples and the number of variables in the computer file. This modified file is available for instructional use, and can be used easily at institutions with access to computer facilities with SPSS. The teaching package consists of a magnetic tape with the modified Comparative Cities SPSS system file (10,000 records), a coursebook with explanations of all variables, a dictionary of all occupational titles and codes appearing in the samples, a sample course syllabus, and some further explanatory material. The cost

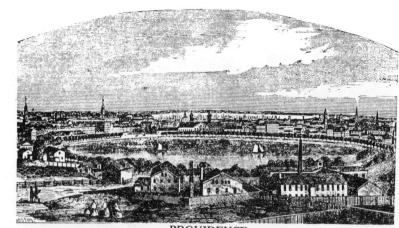

PROVIDENCE

STOCKPORT

PISA

of reproducing the computer tape and other materials is $25. The cost per student in computer time is generally about $50-75 per term. A manual that explains how to code and prepare additional census samples for use with the file is also available. For further information write to me at the Department of History, Brown University, Providence, R.I. 02912.

R.B.L.

COMPARATIVE CITIES: SAMPLE DATA AND QUESTIONS

PERCENT OF MEN AND WOMEN IN EACH AGE GROUP LISTED AS EMPLOYED:
PISA 1841, AMIENS 1851, STOCKPORT 1851, PROVIDENCE 1865*

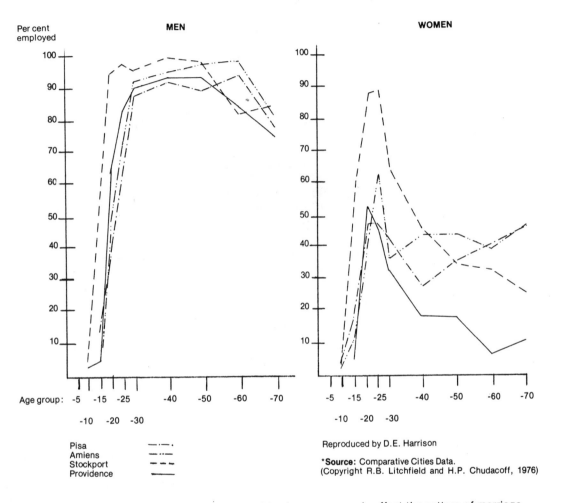

Reproduced by D.E. Harrison

*Source: Comparative Cities Data.
(Copyright R.B. Litchfield and H.P. Chudacoff, 1976)

Pisa — . — .
Amiens — .. —
Stockport — — —
Providence ———

1. Did different employment opportunities for young people affect the pattern of marriage in the industrializing city? Compare Amiens or Pisa with Stockport or Providence.

2. How does the age distribution of women's employment differ between Pisa-Amiens and Stockport-Providence? Did married women work; what effect might this have had on small children?

Using the Comparative Cities Package

In the fall of 1976, along with a colleague at the College of the Holy Cross in Worcester, Theresa McBride taught a one-semester course entitled "Man, Woman, and the Machine: Work and Family During Industrialization," which drew upon the Comparative Cities Data package of Litchfield and Chudacoff.

The course covered topics in the history of industrialization and family patterns, focusing on women. The format varied, including guest lectures, discussions of secondary materials, and student presentations of research conclusions. Each of the eight students presented a major research paper that was based at least in part upon the use of the Comparative Cities data set. The major hinderance was time; no sooner had students learned to use the SPSS programs and become comfortable using the data than the semester was over. But in spite of difficulties, I am convinced of the need for training undergraduates (particularly in the Humanities) in data processing and statistical analysis. The simple experience of using this complicated-seeming machinery gives the student a greater sense of control over the technology that is spreading throughout contemporary society. If for nothing more, the undergraduate should develop an informed cynicism about the uses and abuses of such technology.

But the most exciting part of the course came when students began to trust the conclusions of their own analysis — instead of relying upon the impressions of a secondary source. To the extent that an individual student, for example, began to trust his or her own conclusions about Irish-American family life (based upon the Providence census data) rather more than the suggestions of Andrew Greeley on the topic, the course was a great success.

T. McB.

At the end of each decade of the nineteenth century, enumerators walked door-to-door asking questions for the U.S. Bureau of the Census. Much of the handwritten information they collected is open to the public and readily available for use in classes. These manuscripts, an example of which is reproduced here, personalize the census and connect students to the lives of real individuals in the past.

The first federal censuses, begun in 1790, were merely head counts. The first available census with schedules that include individual names was taken in 1850. Copies of the 1850-1880 census manuscripts are on microfilm in many public and college libraries. If they are not available in your library, copies can sometimes be borrowed from the regional office of the National Archives in Waltham, Massachusetts. They can also be purchased for $12 per reel from the National Archives in Washington. The Census Bureau regularly publishes a list, Federal Population Censuses, 1790-1970: A Catalogue of Microfilm Copies of the Schedule, describing which localities are on each of the reels. The 1890 census was destroyed by fire; the 1900 census does not circulate on microfilm, but is available at the National Archives regional branches. Because government tabulations are so extensive, many class projects are best conducted using the great variety of aggregate results published by the U.S. Bureau of the Census.

Two New England states, Rhode Island and Massachusetts, also conducted their own censuses. The schedules for Rhode Island are more extensive and are available for 1865-1935. Although the published Massachusetts census is a rich source for every decade down to 1925, only the 1855 and 1865 manuscripts survive.

PATRIOT TOWN: Teaching from a Tax List

Bettye Hobbs Pruitt, in consultation with Richard Bushman, both of Boston University, has developed a curriculum about Concord in the Revolution based on the 1771 tax list. Although designed for high school classes, Patriot Town *has also been successfully used by college teachers. It can be obtained by writing to Patriot Town, 207 Bay State Road, Boston, Massachusetts 02215. Copies are $3.25 each ($2.95 for orders of more than 15); an accompanying teacher's manual is also available for $3.50.*

The immediate inspiration for *Patriot Town* was the Massachusetts tax valuation list for 1771, a town-by-town assessment that was the basis for apportionment of the tax burden, both among the towns and among the individuals within each town. It includes the names of all taxpayers (152 towns' lists are extant), the number of adult males in their households, and their taxable property by categories — houses, shops, mills, warehouses, wharfage, merchandise, tillage, pasture, oxen, cows, money lent out at interest, and twenty-two other categories including production per acre of cultivated land. It is an exceptional document, not the least because it permits significant generalizations at every level of analysis. The 1771 valuation has been an important part of several monographs on the demography and social structure of eighteenth-century Massachusetts. At the same time, it is a visually dramatic list that can be read and understood without difficulty. For this reason it seemed ideally suited for introducing into the classroom the excitement of "doing" history — of piecing together bits of evidence, and particularly of trying to understand the past by asking, rather than learning, the answers to questions.

The process by which a curriculum was built around the valuation list consisted literally of working step-by-step through an explication and analysis of the document and translating those steps into classroom exercises. To a great extent it was a process of problem-solving. We devised a system of cards, one for each individual, to be filled out by students, each student becoming responsible for a limited number of cases. The tedium of the recording task could be broken by combining it with an initial analysis of individuals — determining occupation by property owned — and the data could then be sorted and rearranged as needed.

One exercise, for example, calls for comparison of the five largest, five smallest, and five median farms as the basis for a quantitative and, by implication, a qualitative analysis of variation in land distribution. In subsequent sections simple frequency tables are the principal tools, with ranked deciles the basic units of study.

Patriot Town should be useful as a preparation for a study of the student's own town. It is fundamentally a collection of sources, and the framework of exercises and background text are intended to be suggestive, not definitive.

B.H.B.

Adapted from **New England Social Studies Bulletin** (Summer, 1976).

Quantifying School Records

There are many ways that seemingly inert numbers can engage students in the problems and situations of different historical periods. One approach, developed for teachers by the staff at Old Sturbridge Village, builds upon a manuscript record book from a district school in Killingly, Connecticut. Working from this quantitative source, students can imaginatively recreate the life of their age group in the middle of the nineteenth century.

The book itself was at first a confusing collection of teachers' jottings and notes, but Sturbridge has transcribed it and added pertinent U.S. census figures on the students' households along with selections from textbooks then used in the classroom. A curriculum based on this data packet explores daily life in the schools where most nineteenth-century children received their formal education. Students can ask why their predecessors failed to attend school; they can try to understand the subjects that were most important in the 1840's and how they were taught; they can reconstruct the home life of various students, and speculate on its relation to performance in class.

Sturbridge Village has many such curriculum packets for sale to history teachers; among the subjects covered are industry, agriculture, and the family. For information, write to Museum Education Department, Old Sturbridge Village, Sturbridge, Massachusetts 01566.

A LIST of the Polls and of the Estates, Real and Personal of the several Proprietors and Inhabitants of the Town

of *Concord* in the County of *Middlesex* taken pursuant to an Act of the General Court of the Province of the *Massachusetts-Bay*, intitled, *An Act for enquiring into the Rateable Estates of this Province*, passed in the Eleventh Year of his present MAJESTY's Reign, by the Subscribers, Assessors in said Town, duly elected and sworn, Viz. *Ephraim Wood* Jun.*Smith, W. Reeles John Flint*

Men's Names Who are rateable. 207

TEAM ASSIGNMENTS FROM PATRIOT TOWN

1. Draw a graph showing differences in landed wealth in Concord.

    a. Down the lefthand side of a page (or blackboard) mark the horizontal lines to show numbers of acres owned. Use multiples of five (i.e., 0, 5, 10, 15. . .).

    b. Draw ten vertical columns, each of which will represent one of the ten deciles listed in Source E ("Economic Decile List: Concord Taxpayers, 1771").

    c. On the lefthand edge of each column mark with a dot the largest number of acres for that decile. On the right edge mark the smallest number. By connecting these dots you will draw a line that describes the distribution of land in Concord.

    d. In each column draw a horizontal line from the dot on the left edge to the right edge of the column. Next draw a vertical line from the dot on the right edge up to the horizontal line. Shade the triangle created by these lines. The result will resemble a staircase, and the shaded area will show you more clearly the differences in land ownership.

2. Use the data you have assembled to discuss the following questions:

    a. Is landed wealth equally distributed in Concord?

    b. Is most of the land monopolized by the wealthiest people?

    c. Is there a distinct middle class? Is it substantial in size? In property?

    d. Does your evidence suggest cause for social conflict? If so, in what segments of the population might tensions have arisen?

PROCESSING DATA WITHOUT A COMPUTER

Mitchell P. Lichtenberg, Social Studies Director of the Franklin (Massachusetts) Public Schools, offers the following advice on the uses of quantitative history in classrooms.

Ways to deal with large amounts of numerical data existed long before the electronic computer was invented. One such system, the needle sort card, provides an easy means to encode and then retrieve data without any knowledge of programming. The system is simple to operate, is portable, and uses not one watt of electrical power. Needle sort cards do not have the vast storage capacity of computers, nor can they perform lightning quick calculations for the user. But the needle sort system can hold enough data to keep many students busy for a week or more, and the cards permit students to apply many basic quantitative operations.

Needle sort cards contain a series of holes around their edges. These holes, assigned to certain characteristics of an individual or item, are notched or punched out to designate if a particular characteristic applies or does not. A deck of needle sort cards might represent the members of a population or group of items under study. The user selects a characteristic, inserts a knitting needle through the appropriate hole, and lifts the needle. As the deck is raised, cards which contain that characteristic fall from the deck. This sorting operation, when repeated many times, provides a substantial amount of information. Individuals who share common characteristics within a population may be compared with those who do not. Simple 2 x 2 tables are easily generated to help validate hypotheses. The system features a random access procedure releasing users from the

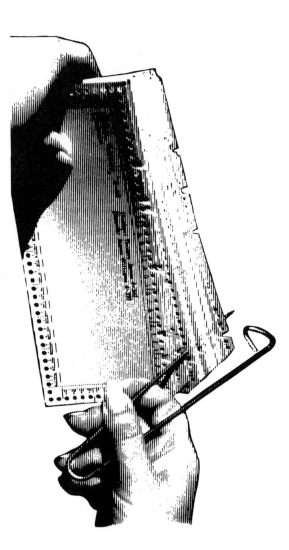

burden of replacing the cards in a specific order.

One example should suffice to demonstrate how students use the needle sort system. During their study of the American colonial period, my high school students became interested in aspects of landholding and migration in the New England villages of the seventeenth century. Using a card deck I had developed around colonial Ipswich, Massachusetts, students were able to pursue many of their hypotheses about who moved and who stayed in this early Puritan community. One pass of the needle through the deck separated landholders from non-landholders. A second pass revealed the migrants from each of these categories. The students counted up the cards, made comparisons, noted findings, and then discussed several other hypotheses which sprang from their discoveries.

Before they had finished, the students had consumed five class periods to probe various aspects of this particular community. Asking questions, creating hypotheses, and searching for results (no matter how unsatisfying or frustrating) seemed far more rewarding to the students than the typical discussion of the reading assignment. Students became active researchers for answers to their own questions. They willingly used my guidelines for accurate research plans and understood the need to avoid unsubstantiated conclusions and overgeneralizations. Along with the enthusiasm came a subtle change in verbal behavior. Statements which once began with "It seems as if . . ." or "It's probably thus and so . . ." now sounded more like "Based on this sample, the evidence indicates . . ." and "What we cannot say at this point is . . .".

While it is clear that quantitative information in this example did not help students to discover motives (why people left Ipswich), the data did give students a better picture of the community's structure (one group of people was more apt to leave than another). More important, students reacted positively to the demands for accuracy and paid careful attention to the issue of what the data could or could not support. During their their last session, students noted the dangers of generalizing from this particular community to the larger world of colonial New England. In a follow-up class I distributed several articles by professional historians which reported findings on the same topics. This not only helped to reinforce the students' tentativeness about their conclusions but also gave them a sense of "sharing" what they had done with the research of others.

It was this sense of participation, even at a rather primitive level, that many students found most rewarding of all. Once

---

Educational Systems Research has several data bank packets for sale: Ward 23, Pittsburgh, 1870-1900; Who Came to the First U.S. Congress?; U.S. Southern Leadership, 1850-1900; and Community in Colonial Massachusetts. All are based on the needle sort system. A do-it-yourself kit is also available. Write: ESR, P.O. Box 157, Shrewsbury, Massachusetts 01545.

---

over the statistical hurdle, teachers of history will discover that quantification well serves the objective of direct student participation in historical research. Until recently, most students at the secondary and undergraduate level learned the product of historical research but little of its process. Attempts by curriculum developers to devise more appropriate materials for historical inquiry have met with limited success.

Primarily this is because documentary evidence requires both a heavy reading load and a sophisticated ability to interpret the written word. Quantified history, while no less complicated at its highest level, can be reduced to simple, straightforward operations which the novice can comprehend. It is in this sense that historical quantification provides an avenue for students to pursue their own research.

M.P.L.

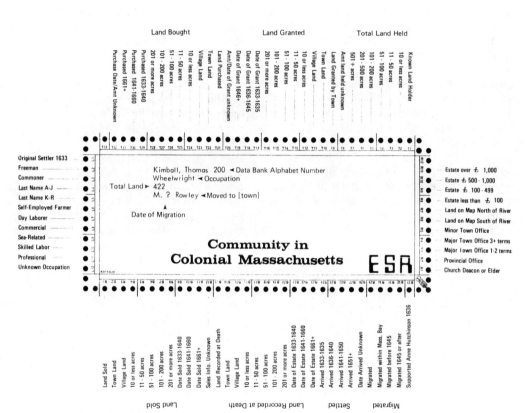

Here is a sample needle sort card of the type described by Mitchell P. Lichtenberg on the previous page. Each group of holes represents a particular characteristic coded on the card (e.g., land held, date of settlement, occupation).

QUANTIFYING FAMILY AND COMMUNITY HISTORY

Robert A. Gross of Amherst College teaches a course on family and community history that combines quantitative with qualitative materials.

Teaching family and community history poses a difficult challenge to the instructor. The subject is intensely relevant, even if technically quite forbidding. A course on family and community speaks directly to the personal concerns of both teacher and student; it emphasizes emotions and experiences common to people everywhere: being children, growing up and raising families, growing old and facing death. And since it stresses the personal and the familiar at a time of rapid social change — indeed, since the recent explosion of interest in family history is a very product of that change — the course must necessarily address the sources and significance of new and troubling developments in family and community life.

My course set out to examine family and community life in America from colonial times to the present and to introduce students to a variety of approaches to the subject. The class began with a brief, despairing look at family life today — a viewing of the first episode of "An American Family," the 1973 televised documentary on the Louds of California, and a reading of Philip Slater's indictment of American life, *The Pursuit of Loneliness* (1970). We then turned to the historical record. First came the beginnings, evolution, and eventual collapse of the patriarchal social order of colonial New England. Then we examined the "modernization" of family and community life and assessed the impact of slavery,

immigration, industrialization, and urbanization on families over the nineteenth and early twentieth centuries. To many of the students the chief value of the course lay in the final paper topic: the construction of a family history. I handed out a questionnaire prepared by the Anonymous Families History Project, discussed techniques of interviewing, and asked students to evaluate their own family histories in the light of the main themes and concepts of the course. The concluding sessions of the course returned to the contemporary scene for another, slightly more hopeful look at the American family and a consideration of alternatives to middle-class nuclear family life.

The course combined qualitative with quantitative analysis. We looked at photographs and novels as sources on community life and took a field trip to Historic Deerfield to study the physical basis of community: architecture, land use, household arrangements. But while family history is ultimately a qualitative enterprise, a study of the emotions and ideas informing attitudes and behavior in different historical settings, it rests firmly upon a structure of quantitative evidence. Students must know something about demography, about family size and structure, about the life cycle, and about social and economic structures in order to comprehend the boundaries and constraints within which families express their intimate life. And all of these subjects involve numbers — the *bête noire* of many, if not most, undergraduates in history courses.

To bridge the gap between the personal and the technical, the course gave students direct experience in doing quantitative his-

tory. I assembled a collection of primary sources on the town of Amherst: genealogies, town meeting records, tax lists, census schedules, town directories, and maps. Assignments in these sources accompanied the readings in secondary historical works. Thus, while students read John Demos's *A Little Commonwealth* (1970), they also reconstituted the founding families of Amherst. In connection with Kenneth Lockridge's *A New England Town* (1970), they studied town meeting records and computed the distribution of wealth in Amherst in 1776. And as they read Richard Sennett's *Families Against The City* (1970), they analyzed pages of the manuscript census of Amherst for 1870. In the weekly lecture, I explained the different methods that could be used to exploit a source; in the weekly seminar, we discussed what the students had found, with special attention to the difficulties and biases involved in using the source. Then we assessed the relative success with which the author of the week's reading had employed similar methods and sources. This mode of teaching requires a good deal of time in assembling and carefully delimiting sources for the students' use. But it proved invaluable for giving them a realistic base from which to criticize the readings and from which to understand what it means to construct an interpretation of the past.

R.A.G.

QUANTO-QUIZ

Relation of Slave Imports to Population of African Descent in the Western Hemisphere, c. 1950 (in thousands)

	Estimated Slave Imports		Estimated population partly or entirely of African descent 1950	
	#	%	#	%
U.S. & Canada	427	4.5	14,916	31.1
Mexico & Central America	224	2.4	342	.7
Caribbean Islands	4,040	43.0	9594	20.0
South America	4,700	50.0	23,106	48.2
	9,391	100.0	47,958	100.0

What can you tell about slavery and Afro-Americans from this chart?

- -

Parish of Colyton, East Devon

Mean intervals (in months) between births of families of four or more children in which the woman married under the age of 30 and survived at least to 45.

Period	0-1st Child	1st-2nd Child	2nd-3rd Child	3rd-4th Child	Penultimate-last child
1560-1646	11.3	25.2	27.4	30.1	37.5
1647-1719	10.3	29.1	32.6	32.1	50.7
1720-1769	11.9	25.1	29.8	32.9	40.6

What do these figures tell you about changes in family life and sexual behavior in seventeenth-century England?

- -

Simplified Returns on the Vote for the Federal Constitution

For	40%
Against	30%
Not Voting	30%

Did a majority favor or oppose the Constitution?

A striking point made by this chart, taken from Philip Curtin's **The Atlantic Slave Trade** (1969), is the rapid population growth among Afro-Americans in the United States and Canada. The U.S. was an unimportant destination for slave traders; fewer than 5% of all slaves shipped here. Yet in 1950, almost one-third of all those of African descent in the Western hemisphere lived in the United States. Since a population's ability to survive and multiply is one measure of its well-being, these statistics may cast doubt on the argument that slavery in Latin America was milder than in the U.S. The data, however, probably indicate more about the disease environments and the economies of the different areas than about the humanity of slaveowners.

A noteworthy feature of this table is the long interval between the penultimate and last births in the middle period (1647-1719). This is characteristic of a community in which people are practicing family limitation. The data here reflect efforts by some couples to prevent the addition of children to their families, despite occasional accidents and reversals of intention. Generally, the example of Colyton indicates the possibility of stabilizing population in pre-industrial Europe without Malthusian disaster. How? The numbers do not say, but miscellaneous non-quantitative evidence elsewhere suggests that abortion, infanticide, and coitus interruptus account for the pattern registered above. See E.A. Wrigley, "Family Limitation in Pre-Industrial England," **Economic History Review** (April, 1966).

There is no right answer for this question. The answer could be "No," since women, Blacks, Indians, and many poor people were not consulted at all. The answer depends on how you define majority and how you qualitatively weight information like "not voting," "no opinion," "don't know," etc. If "not voting" is interpreted as an apathetic acceptance of what most other people are doing, one could say that the 30% not voting agreed with the 40% for the Constitution, so that 70% favored the Constitution actively or passively. Or, if you interpret "not voting" as opposition to change and acceptance of the old status quo, then you could argue that 60% opposed the Constitution actively or passively.

SOURCES FOR QUANTITATIVE CLASS PROJECTS

1. Account books (found at historical societies, the American Antiquarian Society in Worcester, the Baker Library at the Harvard Business School, and local businesses) provide information on wages, profits, employment, business cycles, and other topics in economic history.

2. Church records (local churches, archdiocesan archives) give demographic information for analysis of the social and ethnic characteristics of church members.

3. City directories (public libraries, historical societies, state libraries) provide the names, addresses, and occupations of individual city residents, in addition to listing public officials and businesses. They are especially useful for studying mobility, occupational structure, and the character of neighborhoods.

4. Court records (municipal, county, state, and federal courts) are particularly relevant to the study of crime rates, violence, and property transactions.

5. Dun and Bradstreet credit records (Baker Library at Harvard Business School) go back into the nineteenth century and include information on an individual's loans, bank accounts, other assets, and commercial activities.

6. Land deeds (county courthouse) give the location, acreage, prices, buyers, etc., for each lot in a community. They show population dispersion, urban development, and land use patterns.

7. Tax lists (city halls, historical societies, public libraries) provide detailed information on the wealth of individuals and the value of economic enterprises. Such data can also be grouped by neighborhoods.

8. Vital records (city halls, state archives) which list births, deaths, and marriages have been compiled for all the New England states up to 1850. They are standard sources for studying age distributions, fertility ratios, marriage ages, and life expectancy.

9. Voting statistics (newspapers, election commissions, state archives) make possible analysis of elections by ward or precinct.

10. Wage and price data (Bureau of Labor Statistics, newspapers, state commission reports, advertisements) are invaluable for determining both costs and standards of living for different groups.

Other important quantitative sources include probate records, school records, hospital records, and genealogies. For information on federal and state censuses, see page 103.

Non-American Sources

Quantitative source material for other countries is much less accessible to New England teachers than American material, but the United Nations has published much data on the period since 1948 in the *Demographic Yearbook*, the *United Nations Statistics Yearbook*, and elsewhere. The Population Research Center at the University of Texas has issued a seven-volume *International Population Census Bibliography* (1965-1967) listing published censuses, mostly from the nineteenth and twentieth centuries. To locate a copy of a particular census, one can look in the Library of Congress's *National Union Catalog*, which covers the holdings of major research libraries. Judith Black and Jerry Donovan, *Western European Censuses, 1960: An English Language Guide* (1971), provides explanations of technical terms, classifications, and concepts used in various recent Western European censuses.

Quantifying Non-Numerical Documents

Quantification may enhance even the study of literary and material evidence. The basic procedure is simple: first devise a classification scheme and then count the number of items that belong in the different categories. For example, a class might want to study changing images of women in nineteenth-century women's magazines. First, the class would draw up a list of common stereotypes of women from the period (e.g., piety, submissiveness, domesticity). Then, each student might read and record the incidence of these stereotypes in several short stories from nineteenth-century women's magazines (e.g., **Godey's Lady's Book**, **Ladies Repository**). Finally, the class could compile the results and thus have a measure of how images of women changed over time. A similar approach could be followed for other topics: types of heroes or villains in fiction (age, occupation, ethnic identity, etc.); attitudes toward the professions (stereotypes of doctors, lawyers, clergy).

Newspapers also offer rich material for quantitative investigation. The growth of sports, for example, could be examined by counting the columns devoted to coverage of different kinds of events. A similar approach is applicable to material culture. House styles or gravestone designs can easily be classified, counted, and analyzed by students in collective class projects.

MACAULAY IN THE AGE OF CLIOMETRICS

It might well be asked, need the new quantitative historians learn anything at all about the rhetoric of history? It has been said that some subjects do not lend themselves to dramatic or elegant presentation. True enough, though one should not be too categorical about this. Take, for example, the findings of a recent New Historian who devoted himself for many years to the problem of whether there is to be found any relationship between number of siblings and extent of baldness among the clockmakers of southeastern Ohio between 1823 and 1859. Employing the latest sampling, data-collecting, and computer techniques, he established beyond controversy that 47 per cent of those clockmakers with three or more siblings were totally or partially bald; whereas of those with two or less siblings 49 per cent were totally or partially bald. Those, baldly stated, were his conclusions. But, had he had his Macaulay at his side, he might have phrased them somewhat differently:

As every schoolboy knows, the population of Marietta, Ohio, in 1826 amounted to 1,051 souls. Since that time, what was then a mere hamlet has become a town and grown to a greatness which this generation can only contemplate with pride and wonder. What not so long ago was a peaceful and tranquil village set amidst green fields has become a busy and opulent center of lively manufacturers and commerce, justly famed for its iron and dross castings, its paints and varnishes, its gas engines and ranges, and its household and office furniture. In the year of the Great Exhibition, elderly local inhabitants barely living could recall the building of the first frame house, and the start of the first mail route, when the post left Marietta every Tuesday at noon and arrived at Zanesville every Thursday before dawn. It was in 1851 that the Belpre and Cincinnati railroad became the Marietta and Cincinnati. There were fools in that day as in ours who said that the line from Cincinnati could never extend to Baltimore and Philadelphia. But they were confounded when, on April 9, 1857, the citizens of Marietta heard the cheerful and manly sound of whistle and bell as the first train rumbled in from Chillicothe. Among those who watched its arrival were a few honest farmers who expressed their delight by remarking, in the fashion of rustics everywhere, that the engine gleamed like the head of a bald clockmaker.

As baldness becomes more and more common, brothers and sisters become less and less necessary. Why this should be so we shall state as concisely as possible. As civilization advances, the wearing of hats increases. As a greater number of hats comes into the possession of a greater number of families, more hats will be worn. The more often hats are worn in youth, the greater the loss of hair in middle age. It follows, therefore, as night does day that in the South Eastern portion of Ohio, one of the United States of America, forty-seven per cent of those clockmakers with three or more brothers and sisters were wholly or partly bald, whereas of those with two or less brothers and sisters as great a number as forty-nine percent found themselves in a similar predicament.

John Clive
Harvard University

Excerpted from the **Times Literary Supplement** (March 7, 1975).

APPENDIX

New England has an abundance of historical museums and sites. Many offer only guided tours, but some have elaborate reconstructions and extensive educational programs making use of their research materials, historic buildings, and material artifacts. Although most places with special programs aim at young audiences, there is no reason why students and teachers at the college and graduate level cannot learn from them. Too often college students and teachers fail to utilize potentially educational museums and historic sites in their own localities. The staff at some sites are enthusiastic amateurs, but more museums are actively seeking out experienced teachers and training young people to bring out the full educational possibilities of their resources.

For reasons of space, it is impossible to list every museum, historical society, and historic site in the region. Instead, we have tried to provide a representative sampling of those places offering high school and college programs that go beyond the usual guided tours. A few institutions are described in greater detail because they offer models for the imaginative development of major themes in this book. Museums that currently offer no educational programs may be willing, even eager, to develop them in collaboration with local history teachers.

The Bath Marine Museum (963 Washington St., Bath, Maine 04530) maintains four historic sites located in Bath, the oldest still-active shipbuilding city in the United States. It offers a number of educational programs and lectures related to maritime history. Apprentice, Intern, and volunteer programs enable students to build revivals of turn-of-the-century wooden work boats.

The Bethel Historical Society (Bethel, Maine 04217) offers instruction in old-time crafts, research techniques in local history, and the development of the logging industry. It also trains young people as museum guides and offers an award for the best high-school essay on local history. Publications and a bibliography of local lore are available on request.

The Brockton Art Center (Oak Street, Brockton, Massachusetts 02401) offers imaginative programs at its galleries and in schools through curriculum enrichment kits. One kit on ancient art and life gives background on the formal exhibits, a glossary of terms, ideas for classroom projects, and bibliography. The substance of the kit dwells on the significance of the Nile River cultures, funeral customs, the style of wall-paintings and bas-relief statuary, mummification, cosmetics, artifacts, and the symbolic meaning of hieroglyphs. Many of the same themes, artifacts, and projects are also relevant to the study of Greece, Rome, and their influence throughout the Mediterranean world. One class has used the exhibits and related materials to compose an ancient Egyptian newspaper with text, drawings, comic strips, and a hieroglyphic cross-word puzzle.

The Children's Museum (Jamaicaway, Boston, Massachusetts 02130) has developed curriculum kits and resources for different national and ethnic cultures. For example, the Museum's permanent exhibit on the Japanese Home provides an opportunity for students under the direction of the teaching staff to explore Japanese language, family life, and culture. Similarly, the Museum's East Asian Education Project, offered jointly with the Harvard Language and Area Center for East Asian Studies, arranges a variety of school programs both at the Museum and in the classroom. In conjunction with this program, the Museum offers two in-service courses for teachers, "Teaching about Japan" and "Teaching about China," as well as more general curriculum planning and development services. The Museum has also developed widely-used curriculum kits on children's lives among Native Americans, on the farm, and in Arabia. And a recent grant from the National Endowment for the Humanities will help develop a project on the mixed cultures of South Boston — Italian, Puerto Rican, West Indian, and Irish — near the site of the Museum's new display area on Congress Street Wharf.

The Decordova Museum (Lincoln, Massachusetts 01773) has a staff trained not only in the history and appreciation of many arts and crafts but also in their practice. Teachers interested in the arts of a particular culture can participate in summer workshops that concentrate each year on a different civilization. Also offered during the summer are workshops on art-curriculum planning, on art history and appreciation, and on the practice and history of such crafts as American furniture design and textile arts. Of most direct interest to history teachers in the area is the "Learning Through Art" program, funded by ESEA Title IV C and the Junior League of Boston, Inc., in which volunteer docents, trained by the Museum staff, work with local schools and teachers. Under the direction of Merrie Blocker and Lana Branton, lesson sets are prepared that rely heavily on slides of art and architecture and on artifacts themselves and are coordinated with the social studies curricula of particular schools.

The Essex Institute (Salem, Massachusetts 01970) has a wealth of exhibits and resources in regional history with special emphasis on the maritime industry. For school groups, it has pre-visit packets on its documents, exhibits, historic houses, and artifacts, as well as "outreach" films on the Museum itself, the Revolution, Nathaniel Hawthorne, Salem in the 1890's, Abolitionists, and, of course, witchcraft.

The Danvers Archival Center, located in the basement of the Danvers Historical Society (13 Page St., Danvers, Massachusetts 01923), is probably the first repository in the United States to bring together all of the public and private historic assets of an entire community. With financial support from the Peabody Institute Library and the Historical Society, as well as cooperation from the Town Clerk and other city officials and civic leaders, the Danvers Archival Center is a unique resource for teachers organizing local history projects in the Danvers area. Moreover, it suggests an excellent model that might be imitated in other communities.

The Haffenreffer Museum of Anthropology (Tower St., Bristol, Rhode Island 02809), an adjunct of Brown University, has general exhibits on the cultures of native Americans, with special emphasis on the Indians of southeastern New England and the artifacts of Arctic peoples. The museum offers travelling programs with slides and artifacts, available to schools in Rhode Island and nearby Massachusetts.

Hancock Shaker Village (Box 898, Pittsfield, Massachusetts 01201) offers an excellent look at one of New England's many communal experiments. In addition to lectures and student tours, the Village has been expanding its demonstration craft workshops — spinning, weaving, dyeing, herbal preparations, dairying, woodworking, basketmaking, blacksmithing, and printing. Besides training programs for guides, it runs an internship program for students at Berkshire Community College and Skidmore, and out-reach projects for teachers at the high school and elementary levels.

Heritage Plantation of Sandwich (Grove St., Box 566, Sandwich, Massachusetts 02563) is a diversified museum of Americana with collections that range from military history to horticulture to antique motor cars to folk art. The Museum's Department of Education actively encourages school groups to study the collections by prior appointment, and provides outlines to prepare classes for their visits.

Historic Deerfield (Deerfield, Massachusetts 01342) offers educational programs utilizing the resources of this remarkably well-preserved old Puritan town. The College Visitation Program, for example, enables undergraduate and graduate students to complement regular class instruction by examining the history, life, arts, and material culture of Deerfield. Guided tours are supplemented by lectures, films, slide presentations, and architectural-historical walks. Tours are arranged thematically, according to a class's subject interests, and require advance registration. The Summer Fellowship Program allows undergraduate students a more extended eight-week exposure to Historic Deerfield. This program is intended to encourage young men and women to consider careers in the museum profession or in related fields of historic preservation, American studies, American history, and American art.

The Lowell Museum (560 Suffolk St., Lowell, Massachusetts 01852) has special tours of its facilities for teachers who plan to bring class groups or use the museum's resources for research. The museum's "period" rooms differ from the usual Chippendale-and-Lowestoft arrangements. One set re-creates the living quarters of New England women working in nineteenth-century dormitories owned by the mill company; another set depicts the living conditions of tenement life for immigrant workers. Part of the museum is located in a working textile mill (The Suffolk Company, 1831) where visitors can follow through the whole process of making thread, spinning, and loom weaving. The museum has also received a grant from the Massachusetts Council on the Arts and Humanities to develop three kits for classroom use on immigrants, cotton production, and women.

The Maine State Museum (Augusta, Maine 04333), in conjunction with guided tours of the state house, provides materials and suggestions for a variety of follow-up activities on the history of the region, including a "grandma's trunk" of domestic artifacts, group role-plays, a mock archaeological dig, and an introduction to the intricacies of stencilled wall decoration common to nineteenth-century New England houses.

The Merrimack Valley Textile Museum (North Andover, Massachusetts 01845) collects and exhibits a wide range of artifacts — hand implements, machines, spinning wheels, hand looms, power looms, clothes — which illustrate the history of textile manufacturing. For teachers interested in bringing their classes to the Museum, the education department can arrange special tours emphasizing mechanical technology, social history, or textile design. The Museum also offers programs for the classroom in which a member of the staff presents a slide series on hand and machine processes of woolen manufacturing, a demonstration of spinning and weaving techniques, and suggested guidelines for class projects. Through actual practice with hand tools, students may study household activities of colonial America. Experiments with various kinds of looms, yarns, and fibers allow students to explore contemporary applications of hand weaving. Also available from the Museum are a slide lecture on the industrialization of the lower Merrimack Valley watershed and a slide tape on "daily work" among the textile workers of early twentieth-century Lawrence, Massachusetts.

Minuteman National Historical Park (P.O. Box 160, Concord, Massachusetts 01742) has sites scattered along Battle Road (Route 2A) with a Visitor's Center east of the town center. Reservations are required for special group visits. Programs available at the sites include a comparison of country and city life in colonial times and a role-play debate on boycotting British imports. The Park has films for loan to schools and an environmental history workshop, as well as loan kits on archaeological methods, country history, the equipment of minutemen and British soldiers, and a "grandma's trunk" with ordinary objects for identification and inspection.

The Museum of Afro-American History (Smith Court, Boston, Massachusetts 02114), housed in the old African Meeting House built by free Blacks in 1806, presents a variety of exhibits on Black history, and runs an artist-in-residence program to record Black experience in Boston. In addition, the Museum has laid out a Black Heritage Trail for guided and unguided walking tours of Beacon Hill, showing an early school for Black children, a station on the Underground Railroad, nineteenth-century homes of Black people, and their meetinghouses.

The Museum of Fine Arts (465 Huntington Ave., Boston, Massachusetts 02115), through its Department of Public Education, not only conducts single and multi-visit tours of collections for school groups but also is willing to construct in-depth programs to suit the individual needs of schools, teachers, and students. One such cooperative venture is the American Craftsmanship program, in which the Champlain Middle School in Dorchester and the Museum have for the past two years collaborated to explore the social and cultural history of colonial America.

Mystic Seaport, Inc. (Mystic, Connecticut 06355) is more than a quaint collection of interesting old ships. In association with the University of Connecticut, it offers a summer program in Maritime Studies, with lectures and advanced seminars covering the whole historic development of maritime commerce essential to the region's economy and social experience. During the year, a similar series of courses is conducted in conjunction with Williams College in maritime history, literature, art, oceanography, biology, and uses of the sea. Aside from research and writing, students learn about boat-building, celestial navigation, design, and seamanship. The Seaport gives teacher workshops on the educational uses of the museum's resources and the possibilities of studying culture through maritime artifacts and skills like rowing and fish splitting. For less intensive visits, there are short demonstration courses in sail-making, tarring hemp, scrimshaw, harpooning, and the intricate logistics of old-time whaling.

The New England Historic Genealogical Society (101 Newbury St., Boston, Massachusetts 02215) is the oldest genealogical organization in the country. Formerly used almost exclusively by Brahmins and their admirers, the Society is transforming its periodical **Register** to reflect newer trends in regional, family, and social history. During recent summers it has developed an intensive program at Harvard on the new style of genealogical research, including studies of mobility and demography.

Nook Farm Research Library (77 Forest St., Hartford, Connecticut 06105) includes the houses of Mark Twain and Harriet Beecher Stowe as well as the manuscripts and published writings of these improbable neighbors. The emphasis is obviously on nineteenth-century literature, but the facilities also include resources for studying religion, art, landscape architecture, abolitionism, the arms industry of the Hartford area, and women's suffrage. The Library offers teachers' workshops in museum education, with kits on the Beechers, Stowes, and Twain.

Old Sturbridge Village (Sturbridge, Massachusetts 01566) is an outdoor history museum that recreates the historical environment of a small New England town, complete with houses, school, meeting-house, tavern, store, bank, craft shops, and a working farm. The highly trained staff of the Museum Education Department has developed a number of history teaching resources and programs, several of which are described in other sections of this book. The staff works with teachers who plan to bring classes to its facilities, helping them to plan activities that best fit their classroom needs. Students are encouraged to experience the life patterns of early nineteenth-century New Englanders, to use the same implements and confront the same familial and community issues that such villages actually faced. Through an institutional membership program, school systems can send faculty for intensive summer training programs that utilize the facilities of the Village to develop curriculum materials for their classrooms. A great variety of material and documentary sources as well as complete curriculum kits are available for purchase from the Village. Currently, with the help of an NEH grant, the Village is developing an elaborate program to enhance the place of history in the educational experience of the high school student.

The Olde Courthouse (Rte 6A, Barnstable Village, Massachusetts 02630) maintains a 1772 courthouse and an 1842 Baptist Church. In addition, through a project called "Tales of Cape Cod," the society is developing an historic center to record and preserve oral histories of Cape Cod residents. All the work is shared with the Cape Cod Community College and is available at the library there.

The Park-McCullough House Association, Inc. (North Bennington, Vermont 05257) has developed programs that suggest how imagination and limited resources can provide interesting experiences without elaborate museum facilities or re-creations of whole communities. The house itself was built in 1865 and was lived in by the Hall, Park, and McCullough families for over 100 years, until the Association acquired it in 1968. The families apparently never threw anything away, so that it has valuable collections of family papers, bills, artifacts, and books. During summers, work-study students give tours and write papers based on the house's documents. During the year elementary and high school students pursue educational projects at the house. Two classes have written Victorian plays which have been performed frequently there. Another class did the research, cooking, and preparation for a Victorian meal in the dining room. Shorter role-plays fit in well with the decor and furnishings.

The Peabody Museum (East India Square, Salem, Massachusetts 01970) has rich collections illustrating the history of the China trade. It offers special programs to school groups, consisting of talks illustrated with slides or movies, artifacts, and exhibits in the museum. The Education Department also conducts afternoon workshops on how to use the museum as a teaching tool.

Plimoth Plantation (Box 1620, Plymouth, Massachusetts 02360) attempts to enhance understanding of the seventeenth-century New World, and how it came into being, through three outdoor exhibit complexes combined with special programs and static indoor exhibits. The outdoor, or living, exhibits include Mayflower II; a re-created village set in the year 1627; and a re-created Native American settlement staffed by members of the local Indian community.

The Rhode Island Historical Society (52 Power St., Providence, Rhode Island 02906) sponsors an annual forum on Rhode Island history, publishes a quarterly magazine; in addition to manuscripts and newspaper files, it keeps a complete set of newsfilm reels from local television stations starting as early as 1960 — a source often overlooked by libraries and by historians.

The Salem Maritime National Historical Site (Custom House, Derby St., Salem, Massachusetts 01970) preserves a full working waterfront community in the epoch of whalers, clippers, and the China trade, including warehouses, weighing houses, counting rooms, a West Indies goods store, and mansions of the Derby family. One program for visitors uses role-playing to convey the work experience of porters, runners, sailors, wherrymen, owners, agents, and customs officials.

The Saugus Iron Works National Historic Site (244 Central Street, Saugus, Massachusetts 01906) demonstrates seventeenth-century ironmaking techniques through a reconstruction of the iron works established by John Winthrop, Jr., in the 1640's.

The Shelburne Museum (U.S. Route 7, Shelburne, Vermont 05482), in association with the University of Vermont, offers a series of summer lectures and summer courses on rural America, the New England town before 1800, folk art and decoration, furniture, and other topics. The buildings and exhibits of the museum present the variety of nineteenth-century American life.

Sheldon Art Museum (Middlebury, Vermont 05753) gives tours of its 1829 house, and maintains a library and research center with newspaper files, letters, books, 400 account books, maps, photographs, and 200 scrapbooks with details on almost every important house in the region. It also has a "What Is It?" program available in neighboring schools on portraits, landscape art, silhouette-making, reverse glass painting, kitchen utensils, dolls, and toys.

Slater Mill Historic Site (Roosevelt Ave., P.O. Box 727, Pawtucket, Rhode Island 02862) has restored the first successful cotton textile mill in the country (1793), as well as the Wilkinson Mill where the first American industrial lathe was developed. In addition to a restored house of a millwright, the site offers a travelling exhibition to schools on the history of clothing and manufacture of cotton, wool, and flax, complete with spinners and woolcards and raw wool, as well as demonstrations of the different products achieved through braiding, knitting, and weaving.

Storrowtown Village Museum (Eastern States Exposition Grounds, 1305 Memorial Avenue, West Springfield, Massachusetts 01089) is a "living history" museum that recreates an early nineteenth-century New England suburban village. Popular visits for school groups deal with such topics as the role of children, family life, tools of living, leisure activities, religion, and government in nineteenth-century New England. The Institute of Early American Education, a subsidiary of Storrowtown, is a center for historical study of early New England schooling.

INDEX OF NAMES

DATE DUE

GAYLORD			PRINTED IN U.S.